SAS Publishing

SAS® 9.1.3 XML LIBNAME Engine
User's Guide

The Power to Know.

The correct bibliographic citation for this manual is as follows: SAS Institute Inc. 2004. *SAS® 9.1.3 XML LIBNAME Engine: User's Guide*. Cary, NC: SAS Institute Inc.

SAS® 9.1.3 XML LIBNAME Engine: User's Guide

Copyright © 2004, SAS Institute Inc., Cary, NC, USA

ISBN 1-59047-522-4

SAS Institute Inc., SAS Campus Drive, Cary, North Carolina 27513.

1st printing, July 2004

SAS Publishing provides a complete selection of books and electronic products to help customers use SAS software to its fullest potential. For more information about our e-books, e-learning products, CDs, and hard-copy books, visit the SAS Publishing Web site at **support.sas.com/pubs** or call 1-800-727-3228.

Contents

What's New

Overview

The SAS 9.1 (and later) XML engine imports and exports a broader variety of XML documents. The XMLMAP= option specifies a separate XML document that contains specific XMLMap syntax. The XMLMap syntax tells the XML engine how to interpret the XML markup in order to successfully import an XML document.

Note: This section describes the features of the XML LIBNAME engine in SAS that are new or enhanced since SAS 8.2. △

Details

- □ The "LIBNAME Statement Syntax" on page 83 contains the following new options:
  - □ The ODSRECSEP= option controls the generation of a record separator that marks the end of a line in the output XML document.
  - □ The XMLCONCATENATE= option enables you to import an XML document that contains multiple XML documents, which are concatenated into one file.
  - □ The XMLFILEREF= option enables you to specify a fileref for the XML document that is different from the libref. If the fileref and the libref are the same, you do not need to specify the XMLFILEREF= option or the name of the XML document.
  - □ Beginning in SAS 9.1, the option name XMLSCHEMA= specifies an external file that contains separate schema output.
  - □ The XMLPROCESS= option determines how the XML engine processes character data that does not conform to W3C specifications.
- □ The "LIBNAME Statement Syntax" on page 83 contains the following enhancements:
  - □ The XMLTYPE= option now supports the MSACCESS format type. MSACCESS is the XML format for the markup standards that are supported for a Microsoft Access database.
  - □ In SAS 9.1, you can store and access XMLMaps as metadata objects in a SAS Metadata Repository. The following new metadata options enable you to

      access a particular XMLMap in a specific repository: METAPASS=, METAPORT=, METAREPOSITORY=, METASERVER=, and METAXMLMAP=.

☐ Beginning in SAS 9.1.3, the XMLTYPE= option supports the CDISCODM format type. CDISCODM is the XML format for the markup standards that are defined in the Operational Data Model (ODM) that is created by the Clinical Data Interchange Standards Consortium (CDISC), which conforms to the 1.2 schema specification. The new options FORMATACTIVE=, FORMATNOREPLACE=, and FORMATLIBRARY= are used with the CDISCODM format type to specify transcoding preferences.

☐ The XMLMETA= option specifies whether to include metadata-related information in the exported markup. In SAS 9.1, the values for the XMLMETA= option are changed to DATA, SCHEMADATA, and SCHEMA.

    Note: Prior to SAS 9.0, the functionality of the XMLMETA= option was performed by using the keyword XMLSCHEMA=. In SAS 9.0 (and later), the name of the XMLSCHEMA= option is changed to XMLMETA=. △

☐ In the "XMLMap Syntax Version 1.2" on page 95, the content for the DATATYPE element (which specifies the type of data being read from the XML document for the variable) is changed to conform directly to the XML Schema data types specification. For example, in earlier versions of the DATATYPE element, the form **<DATATYPE>DT-8601</DATATYPE>** was accepted. In version 1.2, the form **<DATATYPE>dateTime</DATATYPE>** is accepted.

☐ Several ISO 8601 SAS formats and informats now support the international standard for the representation of dates and times. See Appendix 1, "ISO 8601 SAS Formats and Informats," on page 113.

☐ Using the LABEL= data set option no longer results in a warning message. However, the XML engine does not persist the information.

☐ SAS XML Mapper (previously named XML Atlas) is a graphical interface that generates or modifies the XML markup for an XMLMap. See "Using SAS XML Mapper to Generate and Update an XMLMap" on page 107.

☐ The new XMLMap Manager (a plug-in used with SAS Management Console) provides centralized management of XMLMaps as metadata objects in a SAS Metadata Repository. See "Using XMLMap Manager to Manage XMLMaps as Metadata Objects" on page 109.

Usage

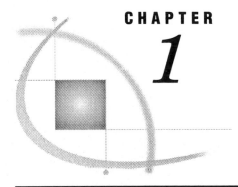

CHAPTER

1

Getting Started with the XML Engine

What Does the XML Engine Do?

The XML engine processes an *XML document*. The engine can

□ export (write to an output file) an XML document from a SAS data set of type DATA by translating the SAS proprietary file format to XML markup. The output XML document can then be

    □ used by a product that processes XML documents.

    □ moved to another host for the XML engine to then process by translating the XML markup back to a SAS data set.

□ import (read from an input file) an external XML document. The input XML document is translated to a SAS data set.

Understanding How the XML Engine Works

Assigning a Libref to an XML Document

The XML engine works much like other SAS engines. That is, you execute a LIBNAME statement in order to assign a libref and specify an engine. You then use that libref throughout the SAS session where a libref is valid.

However, instead of the libref being associated with the physical location of a SAS library, the libref for the XML engine is associated with a physical location of an XML document. When you use the libref that is associated with an XML document, SAS either translates the data in a SAS data set into XML markup or translates the XML markup into SAS format.

Importing an XML Document

To import an XML document as a SAS data set, the following LIBNAME statement assigns a libref to a specific XML document and specifies the XML engine:

```
libname myxml xml 'C:\My Files\XML\Students.xml';
```

Executing the DATASETS procedure shows that SAS interprets the XML document as a SAS data set:

```
proc datasets library=myxml;
```

Output 1.1 PROC DATASETS Output for MYXML Library

```
                                      Directory

            Libref         MYXML
            Engine         XML
            Physical Name  C:\My Files\XML\Students.xml
            XMLType        GENERIC
            XMLMap         NO XMLMAP IN EFFECT


                                              Member
                            #   Name          Type

                            1   STUDENTS      DATA
```

The PRINT procedure results in the following output:

```
proc print data=myxml.students;
run;
```

Output 1.2 PROC PRINT Output of SAS Data Set MYXML.STUDENTS

```
                              The SAS System

         Obs    STATE     CITY         ADDRESS        NAME            ID

          1     Texas     Huntsville   1611 Glengreen Brad Martin     755
          2     Texas     Houston      11900 Glenda   Zac Harvell     1522
```

Exporting an XML Document

To export an XML document from a SAS data set, the LIBNAME statement for the XML engine assigns a libref to an XML document to be created from a SAS data set.

In the following code, the first LIBNAME statement assigns the libref MYFILES to the SAS library that contains the SAS data set Singers. The second LIBNAME statement assigns the libref MYXML to the physical location of the XML document that is to be exported from Myfiles.Singers:

```
libname myfiles 'C:\My Files\';

libname myxml xml 'C:\My Files\XML\Singers.xml';
```

Executing these statements creates the XML document named Singers.XML:

```
data myxml.Singers;
   set myfiles.Singers;
run;
```

Output 1.3 XML Document Singers.XML

```
<?xml version="1.0" encoding="windows-1252" ?>
<TABLE>
   <SINGERS>
      <FirstName> Tom </FirstName>
      <Age> 62 </Age>
   </SINGERS>
   <SINGERS>
      <FirstName> Willie </FirstName>
      <Age> 70 </Age>
   </SINGERS>
   <SINGERS>
      <FirstName> Randy </FirstName>
      <Age> 43 </Age>
   </SINGERS>
</TABLE>
```

SAS Processing Supported by the XML Engine

The XML engine provides input (read) and output (create) processing. However, the XML engine does not support update processing.

The XML engine is a *sequential access* engine in that it processes data one record after the other, starting at the beginning of the file and continuing in sequence to the end of the file. The XML engine does not provide random (direct) access, which is required for some SAS applications and features. For example, you cannot use the SORT procedure or ORDER BY in the SQL procedure with the XML engine. If you request processing that requires random access, a message in the SAS log notifies you that the processing is not valid for sequential access. If this occurs, put the XML data into a temporary SAS data set before you continue. Note that the text of the SAS log messages will refer to invalid access attempts.

Frequently Asked Questions

Is the XML Engine a DOM or SAX Application?

Currently, the XML engine can be either a DOM application or a SAX application, depending on what you are doing:

□ If the format type is either GENERIC (the default) or ORACLE, the XML engine uses a modified Document Object Model (DOM), which converts the document's contents into a node tree. However, for the XML engine, the node tree cannot be queried (traversed).

□ If you are using an XMLMap to import an XML document, the XML engine uses a Simple API for XML (SAX) model. SAX does not provide a random access lookup to the document's contents; it scans the document sequentially and presents each item to the application only one time.

Note that for large XML documents for which you are simply using the format type GENERIC or ORACLE, if you are having resource problems, convert to using an XMLMap, which uses the SAX model.

Does the XML Engine Validate an XML Document?

The XML engine does not validate an input XML document. The engine assumes that the data passed to it is in valid, well-formed XML format. Because the engine does not use a DTD (Document Type Definition) or SCHEMA, there is nothing to validate against.

What Is the Difference between Using the XML Engine and the ODS MARKUP Destination?

Typically, you use the XML engine to transport data, while the ODS MARKUP destination is used to create XML from SAS output. The XML engine creates and reads XML documents; ODS MARKUP creates but does not read XML documents.

Why Do I Get Errors When Importing XML Documents Not Created with SAS?

The XML engine reads only files that conform to the format types supported in the XMLTYPE= engine option. Attempting to import free-form XML documents that do not conform to the specifications required by the supported format types will generate errors. To successfully import files that do not conform to the XMLTYPE= format types, you can create a separate XML document, called an XMLMap. The XMLMap syntax tells the XML engine how to interpret the XML markup into SAS data set(s), variables (columns), and observations (rows).

An exception is the HTML format type, which is supported only for export.

See Chapter 3, "Importing XML Documents," on page 29, Chapter 4, "Importing XML Documents Using an XMLMap," on page 45, "LIBNAME Statement Syntax" on page 83, and Chapter 8, "Creating an XMLMap," on page 95.

Can I Use SAS Data Set Options with the XML Engine?

Use SAS data set options with caution.

Note that while the LABEL= data set option no longer produces a warning message in the SAS log, the XML engine does not persist the information.

Why Does an Exported XML Document Include White Space?

The XML engine is in accordance with the Worldwide Web Consortium (W3C) specifications regarding handling white space, which basically states that it is often convenient to use white space (spaces, tabs, and blank lines) to set apart the markup for greater readability. An XML processor must always pass all characters in a document that are not markup through to the application. A validating XML processor must also inform the application which of these characters constitute white space appearing in element content.

When exporting an XML document, the XML engine adds a space (padding) to the front and end of each output XML element. Here is an example of an exported XML document that shows the white space.

Output 1.4 XML Document with White Space

```
  <?xml version="1.0" encoding="windows-1252" ?>
- <TABLE>
 -- <CLASS>
     <Name> Alfred </Name>
     <Sex> M </Sex>
     <Age> 14 </Age>
     <Height> 69 </Height>
     <Weight> 112.5 </Weight>
    </CLASS>
```

The XML engine does not produce the special attribute **xml:space** for data elements but assumes default processing, which is to ignore leading and trailing white space.

You can remove the white space by specifying the SAS tagset TAGSETS.SASXMNSP. See "Using a SAS Tagset to Remove White Spaces in Output XML Markup" on page 73 for an example.

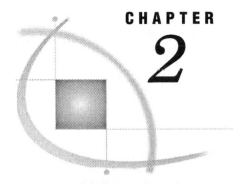

CHAPTER

2

Exporting XML Documents

Understanding How to Export an XML Document

Exporting an XML document is the process of writing a SAS data set of type DATA to an output XML document. The XML engine exports an XML document by translating SAS proprietary format to XML markup.

To export an XML document, you execute the LIBNAME statement for the XML engine in order to assign a libref to the physical location of an XML document to be created. Then, you execute SAS code that produces output such as a DATA step or the COPY procedure.

Exporting an XML Document for Use by Oracle

This example exports an XML document from a SAS data set for use by Oracle. By specifying the Oracle format, the XML engine generates tags that are specific to Oracle standards.

The following output shows the SAS data set MYFILES.CLASS to be exported to Oracle.

Output 2.1   SAS Data Set MYFILES.CLASS to Be Exported for Use by Oracle

Obs	Name	Sex	Age	Height	Weight
1	Alfred	M	14	69.0	112.5
2	Alice	F	13	56.5	84.0
3	Barbara	F	13	65.3	98.0
4	Carol	F	14	62.8	102.5
5	Henry	M	14	63.5	102.5
6	James	M	12	57.3	83.0
7	Jane	F	12	59.8	84.5
8	Janet	F	15	62.5	112.5
9	Jeffrey	M	13	62.5	84.0
10	John	M	12	59.0	99.5
11	Joyce	F	11	51.3	50.5
12	Judy	F	14	64.3	90.0
13	Louise	F	12	56.3	77.0
14	Mary	F	15	66.5	112.0
15	Philip	M	16	72.0	150.0
16	Robert	M	12	64.8	128.0
17	Ronald	M	15	67.0	133.0
18	Thomas	M	11	57.5	85.0
19	William	M	15	66.5	112.0

The following SAS program exports an XML document from the SAS data set MYFILES.CLASS:

```
libname myfiles 'SAS-library'; ❶

libname trans xml 'XML-document' xmltype=oracle; ❷

data trans.class; ❸
   set myfiles.class;
run;
```

1 The first LIBNAME statement assigns the libref MYFILES to the physical location of the SAS library that stores the SAS data set CLASS. The V9 engine is the default.

2 The second LIBNAME statement assigns the libref TRANS to the physical location of the file that will store the exported XML document (complete pathname, filename, and file extension) and specifies the XML engine. The engine option XMLTYPE=ORACLE produces tags that are equivalent to the Oracle8iXML implementation.

3 The DATA step reads the SAS data set MYFILES.CLASS and writes its content in ORACLE XML format to the specified XML document.

Here is the resulting XML document.

Output 2.2 XML Document Exported from MYFILES.CLASS to Be Used by Oracle

```
<?xml version="1.0" encoding="windows-1252" ?>
<ROWSET>
 <ROW>
  <Name> Alfred </Name>
  <Sex> M </Sex>
  <Age> 14 </Age>
  <Height> 69 </Height>
  <Weight> 112.5 </Weight>
 </ROW>
 <ROW>
  <Name> Alice </Name>
  <Sex> F </Sex>
  <Age> 13 </Age>
  <Height> 56.5 </Height>
  <Weight> 84 </Weight>
 </ROW>
 .
 .
 .
 <ROW>
  <Name> William </Name>
  <Sex> M </Sex>
  <Age> 15 </Age>
  <Height> 66.5 </Height>
  <Weight> 112 </Weight>
 </ROW>
</ROWSET>
```

Exporting an XML Document Containing a SAS User-Defined Format

This example exports an XML document from a SAS data set that contains a user-defined format. The only XML format that interprets SAS user-defined formats is the OIMDBM format.

Note: The OIMDBM format type is deprecated in SAS 9. The format type will not be supported in a future release. Functionality will be implemented with a different format type. △

First, the following SAS program defines a user-defined format, creates a simple SAS data set, and prints the contents of the data set:

```
proc format;
   value sex 1='Male'
             2='Female';
run;

data grades;
   input Student $ Gender Test1 Test2 Final;
   format Gender sex.;
   datalines;
Fred 1 66 80 70
Wilma 2 97 91 98
;

proc print data=grades;
run;
```

Output 2.3   PROC PRINT Output for SAS Data Set WORK.GRADES

```
                             The SAS System                              1

            Obs     Student    Gender    Test1    Test2    Final

             1      Fred       Male       66       80       70
             2      Wilma      Female     97       91       98
```

The following code exports an XML document that includes the SAS user-defined format in the metadata-related information:

```
libname trans xml 'XML-document' xmltype=oimdbm xmlmeta=schemadata; ❶

data trans.grades; ❷
   set work.grades;
run;
```

1 The LIBNAME statement assigns the libref TRANS to the physical location of the file that will store the exported XML document (complete pathname, filename, and file extension) and specifies the XML engine. XMLTYPE=OIMDBM specifies the XML format for the standards supported by the Open Information Model, which is the only XML format that recognizes SAS user-defined formats. To generate the appropriate markup for a user-defined format, you must include metadata-related information by specifying XMLMETA=SCHEMADATA.

2 The DATA step reads the SAS data set WORK.GRADES and writes its content in XML markup to the specified file.

The resulting XML document follows. The user-defined format is contained in the metadata-related information in a transformation element using tags **<tfm: Transformation>** and **</tfm: Transformation>**.

Output 2.4 XML Document Containing a SAS User-Defined Format

```
<?xml version="1.0" encoding="windows-1252" ?>
<oim:Transfer xmlns:oim="http://www.mdcinfo.com/oim/oim.dtd"
              xmlns:dbm="http://www.mdcinfo.com/oim/dbm.dtd"
              xmlns:tfm="http://www.mdcinfo.com/oim/tfm.dtd">

   <!-- VersionHeader OimVersion="1.1" OimStatus="Proposal" -->
   <oim:TransferHeader Exporter="SAS Proprietary Software Release
      9.1(9.01.00A0D01262003)"
                       ExporterVersion="9.1"
                       TransferDateTime="2003-01-27T13:23:00" />

   <dbm:ColumnTypeSet oim:id="_7999" name="http://www.w3.org/TR/1998/
      NOTE-XML-data-0105/">
      <dbm:ColumnTypeSetColumnTypes>
         <dbm:ColumnType oim:id="_8000" name="string" IsFixedLength="True" />
         <dbm:ColumnType oim:id="_8001" name="number" />
         <dbm:ColumnType oim:id="_8002" name="int" />
         <dbm:ColumnType oim:id="_8003" name="float" />
         <dbm:ColumnType oim:id="_8004" name="fixed.14.4" />
         <dbm:ColumnType oim:id="_8005" name="boolean" />
         <dbm:ColumnType oim:id="_8006" name="dateTime.iso8601" />
         <dbm:ColumnType oim:id="_8007" name="dateTime.iso8601tz" />
         <dbm:ColumnType oim:id="_8008" name="date.iso8601" />
         <dbm:ColumnType oim:id="_8009" name="time.iso8601" />
         <dbm:ColumnType oim:id="_8010" name="time.iso8601tz" />
         <dbm:ColumnType oim:id="_8011" name="i1" />
         <dbm:ColumnType oim:id="_8012" name="i2" />
         <dbm:ColumnType oim:id="_8013" name="i4" />
         <dbm:ColumnType oim:id="_8014" name="i8" />
         <dbm:ColumnType oim:id="_8015" name="ui1" />
         <dbm:ColumnType oim:id="_8016" name="ui2" />
         <dbm:ColumnType oim:id="_8017" name="ui4" />
         <dbm:ColumnType oim:id="_8018" name="ui8" />
         <dbm:ColumnType oim:id="_8019" name="r4" />
         <dbm:ColumnType oim:id="_8020" name="r8" />
         <dbm:ColumnType oim:id="_8021" name="float.IEEE.754.32" />
         <dbm:ColumnType oim:id="_8022" name="float.IEEE.754.64" />
         <dbm:ColumnType oim:id="_8023" name="uuid" />
         <dbm:ColumnType oim:id="_8024" name="uri" />
         <dbm:ColumnType oim:id="_8026" name="bin.hex" />
         <dbm:ColumnType oim:id="_8027" name="char" />
         <dbm:ColumnType oim:id="_8028" name="string.ansi" />
         <dbm:ColumnType oim:id="_8025" name="bin.base64" />
      </dbm:ColumnTypeSetColumnTypes>
   </dbm:ColumnTypeSet>
```

```
<dbm:Catalog oim:id="_1">
    <dbm:CatalogSchemas>
        <dbm:Schema oim:id="_2">
            <dbm:SchemaTables>

                <!--                                                   -->
                <!-- version 8.2                                       -->
                <!-- this is a new location for the transformation -->
                <!-- desired for supporting multiple table exports -->
                <!--                                                   -->
                <tfm:Transformation>
                    <tfm:TransformationConversion>
                        <tfm:CodeDecodeSet name="SEX">
                            <tfm:CodeDecodeSetCodeColumn oim:href="#_5" />
                                <tfm:CodeDecodeValue name="_TYPE" value="Value" />
                                <tfm:CodeDecodeValue value="1"
                                    DecodeValue="&apos;Male&apos;" />
                                <tfm:CodeDecodeValue value="2"
                                    DecodeValue="&apos;Female&apos;" />
                        </tfm:CodeDecodeSet>
                    </tfm:TransformationConversion>
                </tfm:Transformation>

                <dbm:Table oim:id="_3"
                            name="GRADES"
                            label="Table"
                            EstimatedRows="-1">
                    <dbm:ColumnSetColumns>
                        <dbm:Column oim:id="_4"
                                    name="Student"
                                    Length="8">
                            <dbm:ColumnDataType>
                                <dbm:ColumnType oim:href="#_8000" />
                            </dbm:ColumnDataType>
                        </dbm:Column>
                        <dbm:Column oim:id="_5"
                                    name="Gender">
                            <dbm:ColumnDataType>
                                <dbm:ColumnType oim:href="#_8003" />
                            </dbm:ColumnDataType>
                        </dbm:Column>
                        <dbm:Column oim:id="_6"
                                    name="Test1">
                            <dbm:ColumnDataType>
                                <dbm:ColumnType oim:href="#_8003" />
                            </dbm:ColumnDataType>
                        </dbm:Column>
                        <dbm:Column oim:id="_7"
                                    name="Test2">
                            <dbm:ColumnDataType>
                                <dbm:ColumnType oim:href="#_8003" />
                            </dbm:ColumnDataType>
                        </dbm:Column>
                        <dbm:Column oim:id="_8"
                                    name="Final">
                            <dbm:ColumnDataType>
                                <dbm:ColumnType oim:href="#_8003" />
                            </dbm:ColumnDataType>
                        </dbm:Column>
                    </dbm:ColumnSetColumns>
                </dbm:Table>
```

```
                    <Table oim:href="#_3">
                       <ColumnSetColumns>
                          <Column oim:href="#_4"> Fred </Column>
                          <Column oim:href="#_5"> 1 </Column>
                          <Column oim:href="#_6"> 66 </Column>
                          <Column oim:href="#_7"> 80 </Column>
                          <Column oim:href="#_8"> 70 </Column>
                       </ColumnSetColumns>
                       <ColumnSetColumns>
                          <Column oim:href="#_4"> Wilma </Column>
                          <Column oim:href="#_5"> 2 </Column>
                          <Column oim:href="#_6"> 97 </Column>
                          <Column oim:href="#_7"> 91 </Column>
                          <Column oim:href="#_8"> 98 </Column>
                       </ColumnSetColumns>
                    </Table>

                 </dbm:SchemaTables>
              </dbm:Schema>
           </dbm:CatalogSchemas>
        </dbm:Catalog>

</oim:Transfer>
```

Exporting an XML Document Containing SAS Dates, Times, and Datetimes

This example exports an XML document from a SAS data set that contains datetime, date, and time values. The XML document is generated for the GENERIC format.

First, the following SAS program creates a simple SAS data set and prints the contents of the data set. The variable DateTime contains a datetime value, Date contains a date value, and Time contains a time value.

```
data test;
   DateTime=14686;
   format DateTime datetime.;
   Date=14686;
   format Date date9.;
   Time=14686;
   format Time timeampm.
;

proc print data=test;
run;
```

Output 2.5 PROC PRINT of SAS Data Set WORK.TEST Containing SAS Dates, Times, and Datetimes

```
                          The SAS System                            1

          Obs      DateTime          Date        Time

           1     01JAN60:04:04:46   17MAR2000   4:04:46 AM
```

The following code exports an XML document for the XML format GENERIC that includes the SAS date, time, and datetime information:

```
libname trans xml 'XML-document' xmltype=generic; ❶

data trans.test; ❷
   set work.test;
run;
```

1 The LIBNAME statement assigns the libref TRANS to the physical location of the file that will store the exported XML document (complete pathname, filename, and file extension), and then specifies the XML engine. XMLTYPE= specifies the GENERIC format type, which is the default.

2 The DATA step reads the SAS data set WORK.TEST and writes its content in XML markup to the specified XML document.

Here is the resulting XML document.

Output 2.6   XML Document Using GENERIC Format

```
<?xml version="1.0" encoding="windows-1252" ?>
<TABLE>
   <TEST>
      <DateTime> 1960-01-01T04:04:46.000000 </DateTime>
      <Date> 2000-03-17 </Date>
      <Time> 04:04:46 </Time>
   </TEST>
</TABLE>
```

Exporting an HTML Document

This example exports an HTML document from a SAS data set. With the HTML format type specified, the XML engine generates HTML tags.

Note: The HTML type is deprecated beginning in SAS 9.1.3. The HTML type will not be supported in some future release. Equivalent functionality can be achieved by specifying a tagset. See "Defining and Using a Customized Tagset to Export an HTML Document" on page 76. △

The following output shows the SAS data set MYFILES.CLASS to be exported to an HTML document.

Output 2.7 SAS Data Set MYFILES.CLASS

Obs	Name	Sex	Age	Height	Weight
1	Alfred	M	14	69.0	112.5
2	Alice	F	13	56.5	84.0
3	Barbara	F	13	65.3	98.0
4	Carol	F	14	62.8	102.5
5	Henry	M	14	63.5	102.5
6	James	M	12	57.3	83.0
7	Jane	F	12	59.8	84.5
8	Janet	F	15	62.5	112.5
9	Jeffrey	M	13	62.5	84.0
10	John	M	12	59.0	99.5
11	Joyce	F	11	51.3	50.5
12	Judy	F	14	64.3	90.0
13	Louise	F	12	56.3	77.0
14	Mary	F	15	66.5	112.0
15	Philip	M	16	72.0	150.0
16	Robert	M	12	64.8	128.0
17	Ronald	M	15	67.0	133.0
18	Thomas	M	11	57.5	85.0
19	William	M	15	66.5	112.0

The following SAS program exports an HTML document from the SAS data set MYFILES.CLASS:

```
libname myfiles 'SAS-library'; ❶

libname trans xml 'XML-document' xmltype=html; ❷

data trans.class; ❸
   set myfiles.class;
run;
```

1 The first LIBNAME statement assigns the libref MYFILES to the physical location of the SAS library that stores the SAS data set CLASS. The V9 engine is the default.

2 The second LIBNAME statement assigns the libref TRANS to the physical location of the file that will store the exported HTML document (complete pathname, filename, and file extension) and specifies the XML engine. The engine option XMLTYPE=HTML produces the HTML tags. By default, metadata-related information is not generated.

3 The DATA step reads the SAS data set MYFILES.CLASS and writes its content in HTML format to the specified XML document.

Here is the resulting HTML document.

Output 2.8   HTML Document Exported from MYFILES.CLASS

```
<!DOCTYPE HTML PUBLIC "-//W3C//DTD HTML 3.2 Final//EN">
<HTML>
   <BODY>
      <TABLE border="1" width="100%">
         <TBODY>
            <TR>
               <TD> Alfred </TD>
               <TD> M </TD>
               <TD> 14 </TD>
               <TD> 69 </TD>
               <TD> 112.5 </TD>
            </TR>
            <TR>
               <TD> Alice </TD>
               <TD> F </TD>
               <TD> 13 </TD>
               <TD> 56.5 </TD>
               <TD> 84 </TD>
            </TR>
            .
            .
            .
            <TR>
               <TD> William </TD>
               <TD> M </TD>
               <TD> 15 </TD>
               <TD> 66.5 </TD>
               <TD> 112 </TD>
            </TR>
         </TBODY>
      </TABLE>
   </BODY>
</HTML>
```

Exporting Numeric Values

This example uses a small SAS data set, with a numeric variable that contains values with a high precision. The following SAS program creates the data set with an assigned user-defined format, then exports two XML documents to show the difference in output:

```
libname format xml 'C:\My Documents\format.xml';  ❶

libname prec xml 'C:\My Documents\precision.xml' xmldouble=precision;  ❷

data npi;  ❸
   do n=1 to 10;
      n_pi = n*3.141592653589793;
      output;
   end;
format n_pi f14.2;
run;

data format.dbltest;  ❹
   set npi;
run;
data prec.rawtest;  ❺
```

```
      set npi;
run;

title 'Drops the Precision'; ❻
proc print data=format.dbltest;
   format n_pi f14.10;
run;

title 'Keeps the Precision'; ❼
proc print data=prec.rawtest;
   format n_pi f14.10;
run;
```

1 First LIBNAME statement assigns the libref FORMAT to the file that will store the generated XML document FORMAT.XML. The default behavior for the engine is that an assigned SAS format controls numeric values.

2 Second LIBNAME statement assigns the libref PREC to the file that will store the generated XML document PRECISION.XML. The XMLDOUBLE= option specifies PRECISION, which causes the engine to retrieve the stored raw values.

3 DATA step creates the temporary data set NPI. The data set has a numeric variable that contains values with a high precision. The variable has an assigned user-defined format that specifies two decimal points.

4 DATA step creates the data set FORMAT.DBLTEST from WORK.NPI.

5 DATA step creates the data set PREC.RAWTEST from WORK.NPI.

6 From the data set FORMAT.DBLTEST, PROC PRINT generates the XML document FORMAT.XML, which contains numeric values controlled by the SAS format.

Output 2.9 XML Document FORMAT.XML

```
<?xml version="1.0" encoding="iso-8859-1" ?>
<TABLE>
   <DBLTEST>
      <n> 1 </n>
      <n_pi>                    3.14 </n_pi>
   </DBLTEST>
   <DBLTEST>
      <n> 2 </n>
      <n_pi>                    6.28 </n_pi>
   </DBLTEST>
   <DBLTEST>
      <n> 3 </n>
      <n_pi>                    9.42 </n_pi>
   </DBLTEST>
   <DBLTEST>
      <n> 4 </n>
      <n_pi>                   12.57 </n_pi>
   </DBLTEST>
   <DBLTEST>
      <n> 5 </n>
      <n_pi>                   15.71 </n_pi>
   </DBLTEST>
   <DBLTEST>
      <n> 6 </n>
      <n_pi>                   18.85 </n_pi>
   </DBLTEST>
   <DBLTEST>
      <n> 7 </n>
      <n_pi>                   21.99 </n_pi>
   </DBLTEST>
   <DBLTEST>
      <n> 8 </n>
      <n_pi>                   25.13 </n_pi>
   </DBLTEST>
   <DBLTEST>
      <n> 9 </n>
      <n_pi>                   28.27 </n_pi>
   </DBLTEST>
   <DBLTEST>
      <n> 10 </n>
      <n_pi>                   31.42 </n_pi>
   </DBLTEST>
</TABLE>
```

For the PRINT procedure output, a format was specified in order to show the precision loss. In the output, the decimals after the second digit are zeros. Here is the procedure output.

Output 2.10 PRINT Procedure Output for FORMAT.DBLTEST

```
                    Drops the Precision                    1

              Obs                   N_PI          N

               1            3.1400000000          1
               2            6.2800000000          2
               3            9.4200000000          3
               4           12.5700000000          4
               5           15.7100000000          5
               6           18.8500000000          6
               7           21.9900000000          7
               8           25.1300000000          8
               9           28.2700000000          9
              10           31.4200000000         10
```

7 From the data set PREC.RAWTEST, PROC PRINT generates the XML document
PRECISION.XML, which contains the stored numeric values.

Output 2.11 XML Document PRECISION.XML

```
<?xml version="1.0" encoding="iso-8859-1" ?>
<TABLE>
   <RAWTEST>
      <n rawvalue="QRAAAAAAAAA="> 1 </n>
      <n_pi rawvalue="QTJD9qiIWjA=">          3.14 </n_pi>
   </RAWTEST>
   <RAWTEST>
      <n rawvalue="QSAAAAAAAAA="> 2 </n>
      <n_pi rawvalue="QWSH7VEQtGA=">          6.28 </n_pi>
   </RAWTEST>
   <RAWTEST>
      <n rawvalue="QTAAAAAAAAA="> 3 </n>
      <n_pi rawvalue="QZbL4/mZDpA=">          9.42 </n_pi>
   </RAWTEST>
   <RAWTEST>
      <n rawvalue="QUAAAAAAAAA="> 4 </n>
      <n_pi rawvalue="QckP2qIhaMA=">          12.57 </n_pi>
   </RAWTEST>
   <RAWTEST>
      <n rawvalue="QVAAAAAAAAA="> 5 </n>
      <n_pi rawvalue="QftT0UqpwvA=">          15.71 </n_pi>
   </RAWTEST>
   <RAWTEST>
      <n rawvalue="QWAAAAAAAAA="> 6 </n>
      <n_pi rawvalue="QhLZfH8zIdI=">          18.85 </n_pi>
   </RAWTEST>
   <RAWTEST>
      <n rawvalue="QXAAAAAAAAA="> 7 </n>
      <n_pi rawvalue="QhX9u+m7p3U=">          21.99 </n_pi>
   </RAWTEST>
   <RAWTEST>
      <n rawvalue="QYAAAAAAAAA="> 8 </n>
      <n_pi rawvalue="Qhkh+1RELRg=">          25.13 </n_pi>
   </RAWTEST>
   <RAWTEST>
      <n rawvalue="QZAAAAAAAAA="> 9 </n>
      <n_pi rawvalue="QhxGOr7Msrs=">          28.27 </n_pi>
   </RAWTEST>
   <RAWTEST>
      <n rawvalue="QaAAAAAAAAA="> 10 </n>
      <n_pi rawvalue="Qh9qeilVOF4=">          31.42 </n_pi>
   </RAWTEST>
</TABLE>
```

For the PRINT procedure output, a format was specified in order to show the retained precision. Here is the procedure output.

Output 2.12 PRINT Procedure Output from PREC.RAWTEST

```
                    Keeps the Precision        2

           Obs                N_PI           N

            1           3.1415926536          1
            2           6.2831853072          2
            3           9.4247779608          3
            4          12.5663706144          4
            5          15.7079632679          5
            6          18.8495559215          6
            7          21.9911485751          7
            8          25.1327412287          8
            9          28.2743338823          9
           10          31.4159265359         10
```

Exporting an XML Document with Separate Metadata

This example exports an XML document from a SAS data set and specifies a separate file to contain metadata-related information.

Because this example illustrates using the options XMLMETA= and XMLSCHEMA=, which are available for the MSACCESS format type, the example uses a SAS data set that was created from a Microsoft Access database.

The following SAS program exports an XML document from the SAS data set MYFILES.SUPPLIERS:

```
libname input 'c:\My Documents\myfiles'; ❶

filename xsd 'c:\My Documents\XML\suppliers.xsd'; ❷

libname output xml 'c:\My Documents\XML\suppliers.xml' xmltype=msaccess
   xmlmeta=schemadata xmlschema=xsd'; ❸

data output.suppliers; ❹
   set input.suppliers;
run;
```

1 The first LIBNAME statement assigns the libref INPUT to the physical location of the SAS library that stores the SAS data set SUPPLIERS.

2 The FILENAME statement assigns the fileref XSD to the physical location of the separate external file that will contain the metadata-related information.

3 The second LIBNAME statement assigns the libref OUTPUT to the physical location of the file that will store the exported XML document (complete pathname, filename, and file extension) and specifies the XML engine. The engine options

   □ XMLTYPE=MSACCESS supports the markup standards for a Microsoft Access database.

   □ XMLMETA=SCHEMADATA specifies to include both data content and metadata-related information in the exported markup.

   □ XMLSCHEMA= specifies the fileref that is assigned, in the previous FILENAME statement, to the separate external file that will contain the metadata-related information.

4 The DATA step reads the SAS data set INPUT.SUPPLIERS and writes its data content in Microsoft Access database XML format to the XML document Suppliers.XML, then writes the metadata information to the separate external file Suppliers.XSD.

Here is part of the resulting XML document.

Output 2.13 XML Document Suppliers.XML

```xml
<?xml version="1.0" encoding="windows-1252" ?>
    <dataroot  xmlns:xs="http://www.w3.org/2001/XMLSchema"
               xmlns:od="urn:schemas-microsoft-com:officedata">
               xs:noNamespaceSchemaLocation="SUPPLIERS.xsd">
        <SUPPLIERS>
            <SupplierID>1</SupplierID>
            <CompanyName>Exotic Flowers</CompanyName>
            <ContactName>Charlotte Smith</ContactName>
            <ContactTitle>Purchasing Manager</ContactTitle>
            <Address>49 Franklin St.</Address>
            <City>London</City>
            <Region/>
            <PostalCode>EC1 4SD</PostalCode>
            <Country>UK</Country>
            <Phone>(272) 444-2222</Phone>
            <Fax/>
            <HomePage/>
        </SUPPLIERS>
        <SUPPLIERS>
            <SupplierID>2</SupplierID>
            <CompanyName>New Orleans Cajun Foods</CompanyName>
            <ContactName>Shelley Martin</ContactName>
            <ContactTitle>Order Administrator</ContactTitle>
            <Address>P.O. Box 78934</Address>
            <City>New Orleans</City>
            <Region>LA</Region>
            <PostalCode>70117</PostalCode>
            <Country>USA</Country>
            <Phone>(512) 284-3677</Phone>
            <Fax/>
            <HomePage>#MYCAJUN.HTM#</HomePage>
        </SUPPLIERS>
            .
            .
            .
    </dataroot>
```

And here is the separate metadata information.

Output 2.14 Separate Metadata Information Suppliers.XSD

```xml
<?xml version="1.0" encoding="windows-1252" ?>
<xs:schema xmlns:xs="http://www.w3.org/2001/XMLSchema"
           xmlns:od="urn:schemas-microsoft-com:officedata">
    <xs:element name="dataroot">
        <xs:complexType>
            <xs:sequence>
                <xs:element ref="SUPPLIERS"  minOccurs="0" maxOccurs="unbounded" />
            </xs:sequence>
        </xs:complexType>
    </xs:element>
    <xs:element name="SUPPLIERS">
        <xs:complexType>
            <xs:sequence>
                <xs:element name="SupplierID" minOccurs="0"
                 od:jetType="double" od:sqlSType="double" type="xs:double" />
                <xs:element name="CompanyName" minOccurs="0"
                 od:jetType="text" od:sqlSType="nvarchar">
                    <xs:simpleType>
                        <xs:restriction base="xs:string">
                            <xs:maxLength value="40" />
                        </xs:restriction>
                    </xs:simpleType>
                </xs:element>
                <xs:element name="ContactName" minOccurs="0"
                 od:jetType="text" od:sqlSType="nvarchar">
                    <xs:simpleType>
                        <xs:restriction base="xs:string">
                            <xs:maxLength value="30" />
                        </xs:restriction>
                    </xs:simpleType>
                </xs:element>
                <xs:element name="ContactTitle" minOccurs="0"
                 od:jetType="text" od:sqlSType="nvarchar">
                    <xs:simpleType>
                        <xs:restriction base="xs:string">
                            <xs:maxLength value="30" />
                        </xs:restriction>
                    </xs:simpleType>
                </xs:element>
                <xs:element name="Address" minOccurs="0"
                 od:jetType="text" od:sqlSType="nvarchar">
                    <xs:simpleType>
                        <xs:restriction base="xs:string">
                            <xs:maxLength value="60" />
                        </xs:restriction>
                    </xs:simpleType>
                </xs:element>
```

```
<xs:element name="City" minOccurs="0"
            od:jetType="text" od:sqlSType="nvarchar">
            <xs:simpleType>
                <xs:restriction base="xs:string">
                    <xs:maxLength value="15" />
                </xs:restriction>
            </xs:simpleType>
        </xs:element>
        <xs:element name="Region" minOccurs="0"
         od:jetType="text" od:sqlSType="nvarchar">
            <xs:simpleType>
                <xs:restriction base="xs:string">
                    <xs:maxLength value="15" />
                </xs:restriction>
            </xs:simpleType>
        </xs:element>
        <xs:element name="PostalCode" minOccurs="0"
         od:jetType="text" od:sqlSType="nvarchar">
            <xs:simpleType>
                <xs:restriction base="xs:string">
                    <xs:maxLength value="10" />
                </xs:restriction>
            </xs:simpleType>
        </xs:element>
        <xs:element name="Country" minOccurs="0"
         od:jetType="text" od:sqlSType="nvarchar">
            <xs:simpleType>
                <xs:restriction base="xs:string">
                    <xs:maxLength value="15" />
                </xs:restriction>
            </xs:simpleType>
        </xs:element>
        <xs:element name="Phone" minOccurs="0"
         od:jetType="text" od:sqlSType="nvarchar">
            <xs:simpleType>
                <xs:restriction base="xs:string">
                    <xs:maxLength value="24" />
                </xs:restriction>
            </xs:simpleType>
        </xs:element>
        <xs:element name="Fax" minOccurs="0"
         od:jetType="text" od:sqlSType="nvarchar">
            <xs:simpleType>
                <xs:restriction base="xs:string">
                    <xs:maxLength value="24" />
                </xs:restriction>
            </xs:simpleType>
        </xs:element>
        <xs:element name="HomePage" minOccurs="0"
         od:jetType="text" od:sqlSType="nvarchar">
            <xs:simpleType>
                <xs:restriction base="xs:string">
                    <xs:maxLength value="256" />
                </xs:restriction>
            </xs:simpleType>
        </xs:element>
    </xs:sequence>
  </xs:complexType>
 </xs:element>
</xs:schema>
```

Exporting an XML Document in CDISC ODM Format

This example exports the SAS data set that was imported in "Importing a CDISC ODM Document" on page 39 back to an XML document that is in CDISC ODM format. Because the CDISCODM format type is specified, the XML engine generates tags that are specific to the CDISC Operational Data Model.

The following SAS program exports an XML document from the SAS data set ODM.AE:

```
filename output 'C:\myoutput.xml';❶
libname  output xml xmltype=CDISCODM formatactive=yes;❷

data output.AE2;
   set odm.AE;
run;
```

1 The FILENAME statement assigns the fileref OUTPUT to the physical location of the external file to which the exported information will be written (complete pathname, filename, and file extension).

2 The LIBNAME statement specifies the fileref OUTPUT as the output location and specifies the XML engine. It includes the following engine options:

   □ XMLTYPE=CDISCODM supports the markup standards for CDISC ODM 1.2.

   □ FORMATACTIVE=YES specifies to convert SAS formats to the corresponding CDISC ODM CodeList elements.

The output is the same as the XML document that is shown in "Example CDISC ODM Document" on page 129.

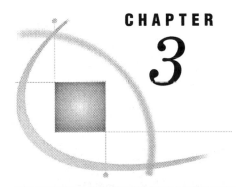

CHAPTER

3

Importing XML Documents

Understanding How to Import an XML Document

Importing an XML document is the process of reading an external XML document as a SAS data set. The XML engine translates the input XML document to the SAS proprietary file format.

To import an XML document, you execute the LIBNAME statement for the XML engine in order to assign a libref to the physical location of an existing XML document. Then, you execute SAS code to access the XML document as a SAS data set.

Importing an XML Document Using the GENERIC Format Type

This example imports the following XML document, which conforms to the physical structure for the GENERIC format type. For information about the required physical structure, see "Understanding the Required Physical Structure for an XML Document to Be Imported Using the GENERIC Format Type" on page 45.

```
<?xml version="1.0" encoding="windows-1252" ?>
<TABLE>
   <CLASS>
      <Name> Alfred </Name>
      <Sex> M </Sex>
      <Age> 14 </Age>
      <Height> 69 </Height>
      <Weight> 112.5 </Weight>
   </CLASS>
   <CLASS>
      <Name> Alice </Name>
      <Sex> F </Sex>
      <Age> 13 </Age>
```

```
      <Height> 56.5 </Height>
      <Weight> 84 </Weight>
   </CLASS>

      .
      .
      .

   <CLASS>
      <Name> William </Name>
      <Sex> M </Sex>
      <Age> 15 </Age>
      <Height> 66.5 </Height>
      <Weight> 112 </Weight>
   </CLASS>
</TABLE>
```

The following SAS program translates the XML markup to SAS proprietary format:

```
libname trans xml 'XML-document'; ❶

libname myfiles 'SAS-library'; ❷

data myfiles.class; ❸
   set trans.class;
run;
```

1 The first LIBNAME statement assigns the libref TRANS to the physical location of the XML document (complete pathname, filename, and file extension), and specifies the XML engine. By default, the XML engine expects GENERIC format.

2 The second LIBNAME statement assigns the libref MYFILES to the physical location of the SAS library that will store the resulting SAS data set. The V9 engine is the default.

3 The DATA step reads the XML document and writes its content in SAS proprietary format.

Issuing the PRINT procedure produces the output for the data set that was translated from the XML document:

```
proc print data=myfiles.class;
run;
```

Output 3.1 PROC PRINT Output for MYFILES.CLASS

```
                     The SAS System                       1

        Obs    WEIGHT     HEIGHT       AGE    SEX    NAME

          1    112.5       69.0         14     M     Alfred
          2     84.0       56.5         13     F     Alice
          3     98.0       65.3         13     F     Barbara
          4    102.5       62.8         14     F     Carol
          5    102.5       63.5         14     M     Henry
          6     83.0       57.3         12     M     James
          7     84.5       59.8         12     F     Jane
          8    112.5       62.5         15     F     Janet
          9     04.0       62.5         13     M     Jeffrey
         10     99.5       59.0         12     M     John
         11     50.5       51.3         11     F     Joyce
         12     90.0       64.3         14     F     Judy
         13     77.0       56.3         12     F     Louise
         14    112.0       66.5         15     F     Mary
         15    150.0       72.0         16     M     Philip
         16    128.0       64.8         12     M     Robert
         17    133.0       67.0         15     M     Ronald
         18     85.0       57.5         11     M     Thomas
         19    112.0       66.5         15     M     William
```

Importing an XML Document with Numeric Values

This example imports the XML document PRECISION.XML, which was exported in "Exporting Numeric Values" on page 18. This example illustrates how you can change the behavior for importing numeric values.

The first SAS program imports the XML document using the default behavior, which retrieves PCDATA from the element:

```
libname default xml 'C:\My Documents\precision.xml';


title 'Default Method';
proc print data=default.rawtest;
   format n_pi f14.10;
run;
```

The result of the import is the SAS data set DEFAULT.RAWTEST.

Output 3.2 PROC PRINT of Data Set DEFAULT.RAWTEST

```
                 Default Method                1

        Obs          N_PI             N

          1     3.1400000000          1
          2     6.2800000000          2
          3     9.4200000000          3
          4    12.5700000000          4
          5    15.7100000000          5
          6    18.8500000000          6
          7    21.9900000000          7
          8    25.1300000000          8
          9    28.2700000000          9
         10    31.4200000000         10
```

The second SAS program imports the XML document using the XMLDOUBLE= option in order to change the behavior, which retrieves the value from the rawdata= attribute in the element:

```
libname new xml 'C:\My Documents\precision.xml' xmldouble=precision;

title 'Precision Method';
proc print data=new.rawtest;
   format n_pi f14.10;
run;
```

The result of the import is SAS data set NEW.RAWTEST.

Output 3.3   PROC PRINT of Data Set NEW.RAWTEST

```
                    Precision Method                    2

          Obs               N_PI             N

            1         3.1415926536           1
            2         6.2831853072           2
            3         9.4247779608           3
            4        12.5663706144           4
            5        15.7079632679           5
            6        18.8495559215           6
            7        21.9911485751           7
            8        25.1327412287           8
            9        28.2743338823           9
           10        31.4159265359          10
```

Importing an XML Document with Non-Escaped Character Data

W3C specifications (section 4.6 Predefined Entities) state that for character data, certain characters such as the left angle bracket (<), the ampersand (&), and the apostrophe (') must be escaped using character references or strings like **<**, **&**, and **'**. For example, to allow attribute values to contain both single and double quotation marks, the apostrophe or single-quotation character (') can be represented as **'** and the double-quotation character (") as **"**.

To import an XML document that contains non-escaped characters, you can specify the LIBNAME statement option XMLPROCESS=RELAX in order for the XML engine to accept character data that does not conform to W3C specifications. That is, non-escaped characters like the apostrophe, double quotation marks, and the ampersand are accepted in character data.

Note: Use XMLPROCESS=RELAX cautiously. If an XML document consists of non-escaped characters, the content is not standard XML construction. The option is provided for convenience, not to encourage invalid XML format. △

This example imports the following XML document named Relax.XML, which contains non-escaped character data:

```
<?xml version="1.0" ?>
<RELAX>
   <CHARS>
      <accept>OK</accept>
      <status>proper escape sequence</status>
```

```
        <ampersand>&amp;</ampersand>
        <squote>&apos;</squote>
        <dquote>&quot;</dquote>
        <less>&lt;</less>
        <greater>&gt;</greater>
    </CHARS>
    <CHARS>
        <accept>OK</accept>
        <status>unescaped character in CDATA</status>
        <ampersand><![CDATA[Abbott & Costello] ]></ampersand>
        <squote><![CDATA[Logan's Run] ]></squote>
        <dquote><![CDATA[This is "realworld" stuff] ]></dquote>
        <less><![CDATA[ e <pi ] ]></less>
        <greater><![CDATA[ pen > sword ] ]></greater>
    </CHARS>

    <CHARS>
        <accept>NO</accept>
        <status>single unescaped character</status>
        <ampersand>&</ampersand>
        <squote>'</squote>
        <dquote>"</dquote>
        <!-- purposely left out the less tag here -->
        <greater/>
    </CHARS>
    <CHARS>
        <accept>NO</accept>
        <status>unescaped character in string</status>
        <ampersand>Dunn & Bradstreet</ampersand>
        <squote>Isn't this silly?</squote>
        <dquote>Quoth the raven, "Nevermore!"</dquote>
        <less></less>
        <!-- purposely left out the greater tag here -->
    </CHARS>
</RELAX>
```

First, using the default XML engine behavior, which expects XML markup to conform to W3C specifications, the following SAS program imports only the first two observations, which contain valid XML markup, and produces errors for the last two records, which contain non-escaped characters:

```
libname relax xml 'c:\My Documents\XML\relax.xml';


proc print data=relax.chars;
run;
```

Output 3.4 SAS Log Output

```
ERROR: There is an illegal character in the entity name.
       encountered during XMLInput parsing
       occurred at or near line 24, column 22
NOTE: There were 2 observations read from the data set RELAX.CHARS.
```

Specifying the LIBNAME statement option XMLPROCESS=RELAX enables the XML engine to import the XML document:

```
libname relax xml 'c:\My Documents\XML\relax.xml' xmlprocess=relax;

proc print data=relax.chars;
run;
```

Output 3.5 PROC PRINT Output

```
                               The SAS System                                    1

Obs    GREATER         LESS       DQUOTE                        SQUOTE

 1     >               <          "                             '
 2     pen > sword     e < pi     This is "realworld" stuff     Logan's Run
 3                                "                             '
 4                                Quoth the raven, "Nevermore!" Isn't this silly?


Obs    AMPERSAND            STATUS                      ACCEPT

 1     &                    proper escape sequence        OK
 2     Abbott & Costello    unescaped character in CDATA  OK
 3     &                    single unescaped character    NO
 4     Dunn & Bradstreet    unescaped character in string NO
```

Importing an XML Document Created by Microsoft Access

This example imports the following XML document, which was created from a Microsoft Access database. Because the XML document contains an embedded XML schema, you must specify the MSACCESS format type rather than the default GENERIC format type. MSACCESS obtains a variable's attributes from the embedded schema.

```
<?xml version="1.0" encoding="UTF-8"?>
<root xmlns:xsd="http://www.w3.org/2000/10/XMLSchema"
  xmlns:od="urn:schemas-microsoft-com:officedata">
<xsd:schema>
<xsd:element name="dataroot">
<xsd:complexType>
<xsd:choice maxOccurs="unbounded">
<xsd:element ref="Suppliers"/>
</xsd:choice>
</xsd:complexType>
</xsd:element>
<xsd:element name="Suppliers">
<xsd:annotation>
<xsd:appinfo>
<od:index index-name="PrimaryKey" index-key="SupplierID " primary="yes"
    unique="yes" clustered="no"/>
<od:index index-name="CompanyName" index-key="CompanyName " primary="no"
    unique="no" clustered="no"/>
<od:index index-name="PostalCode" index-key="PostalCode " primary="no"
    unique="no" clustered="no"/>
</xsd:appinfo>
</xsd:annotation>
```

```
<xsd:complexType>
<xsd:sequence>
<xsd:element name="SupplierID" od:jetType="autonumber" od:sqlSType="int"
    od:autoUnique="yes" od:nonNullable="yes">
<xsd:simpleType>
<xsd:restriction base="xsd:integer"/>
</xsd:simpleType>
</xsd:element>
<xsd:element name="CompanyName" minOccurs="0" od:jetType="text"
    od:sqlSType="nvarchar">
<xsd:simpleType>
<xsd:restriction base="xsd:string">
<xsd:maxLength value="40"/>
</xsd:restriction>
</xsd:simpleType>
</xsd:element>
<xsd:element name="ContactName" minOccurs="0" od:jetType="text"
    od:sqlSType="nvarchar">
<xsd:simpleType>
<xsd:restriction base="xsd:string">
<xsd:maxLength value="30"/>
</xsd:restriction>
</xsd:simpleType>
</xsd:element>
    .
    .
    .
</xsd:sequence>
</xsd:complexType>
</xsd:element>
</xsd:schema>
<dataroot xmlns:xsi="http://www.w3.org/2000/10/XMLSchema-instance">
<Suppliers>
<SupplierID>1</SupplierID>
<CompanyName>Exotic Flowers</CompanyName>
<ContactName>Charlotte Smith</ContactName>
<ContactTitle>Purchasing Manager</ContactTitle>
<Address>49 Franklin St.</Address>
<City>London</City>
<PostalCode>EC1 4SD</PostalCode>
<Country>UK</Country>
<Phone>(272) 444-2222</Phone>
</Suppliers>
<Suppliers>
<SupplierID>2</SupplierID>
<CompanyName>New Orleans Cajun Foods</CompanyName>
<ContactName>Shelley Martin</ContactName>
<ContactTitle>Order Administrator</ContactTitle>
<Address>P.O. Box 78934</Address>
<City>New Orleans</City>
<Region>LA</Region>
<PostalCode>70117</PostalCode>
<Country>USA</Country>
<Phone>(512) 284-3677</Phone>
```

```
<HomePage>#MYCAJUN.HTM#</HomePage>
</Suppliers>
       .
       .
       .
</dataroot>
</root>
```

The following SAS program interprets the XML document as a SAS data set:

```
libname access xml '/u/myid/myfiles/suppliers.xml' xmltype=msaccess ❶
    xmlmeta=schemadata; ❶

proc print data=access.suppliers (obs=2); ❷
    var companyname contactname;
run;
```

1 The LIBNAME statement assigns the libref ACCESS to the physical location of the XML document (complete pathname, filename, and file extension), and specifies the XML engine. By default, the XML engine expects GENERIC format, so you must include the XMLTYPE= option in order to read the XML document in MSACCESS format and to obtain a variable's attributes from the embedded schema. The option XMLMETA=SCHEMADATA specifies to import both data and metadata-related information from the input XML document.

2 The PRINT procedure produces the output. The procedures uses the OBS= data set option to print only the first two observations and the VAR statement to print only specific variables (columns).

Output 3.6   PROC PRINT Output for ACCESS.SUPPLIERS

```
                        The SAS System                                    1

Obs    COMPANYNAME                          CONTACTNAME

 1     Exotic Flowers                       Charlotte Smith
 2     New Orleans Cajun Foods              Shelley Martin
```

Using PROC CONTENTS, the output displays the file's attributes as well as the attributes of each interpreted column (variable), such as the variable's type and length, which are obtained from the embedded XML schema. Without the embedded XML schema, the results for the attributes would be default values.

```
proc contents data=access.suppliers;
run;
```

Output 3.7 PROC CONTENTS Output for ACCESS.SUPPLIERS

```
                              The SAS System                          2

                           The CONTENTS Procedure

      Data Set Name      ACCESS.SUPPLIERS    Observations          .
      Member Type        DATA                Variables             12
      Engine             XML                 Indexes               0
      Created            .                   Observation Length    0
      Last Modified      .                   Deleted Observations  0
      Protection                             Compressed            NO
      Data Set Type                          Sorted                NO
      Label
      Data Representation  Default
      Encoding             Default


                Alphabetic List of Variables and Attributes

       #    Variable      Type    Len    Format    Informat    Label

       5    Address       Char    60     $60.      $60.        Address
       6    City          Char    15     $15.      $15.        City
       2    CompanyName   Char    40     $40.      $40.        CompanyName
       3    ContactName   Char    30     $30.      $30.        ContactName
       4    ContactTitle  Char    30     $30.      $30.        ContactTitle
       9    Country       Char    15     $15.      $15.        Country
      11    Fax           Char    24     $24.      $24.        Fax
      12    HomePage      Char    256    $256.     $256.       HomePage
      10    Phone         Char    24     $24.      $24.        Phone
       8    PostalCode    Char    10     $10.      $10.        PostalCode
       7    Region        Char    15     $15.      $15.        Region
       1    SupplierID    Num     8      F8.       F8.         SupplierID
```

Importing Concatenated XML Documents

For a file that is a concatenation of multiple XML documents, you can use the XML engine to import the file. To import concatenated XML documents, simply specify the LIBNAME statement option XMLCONCATENATE=YES.

Note: Use XMLCONCATENATE=YES cautiously. If an XML document consists of concatenated XML documents, the content is not standard XML construction. The option is provided for convenience, not to encourage invalid XML format. △

This example imports the following file named ConcatStudents.XML, which consists of two XML documents:

```
<?xml version="1.0" ?>
<LIBRARY>
   <STUDENTS>
      <ID>1345</ID>
      <NAME>Linda Kay</NAME>
      <SCHOOL>Bellaire</SCHOOL>
      <CITY>Houston</CITY>
   </STUDENTS>
   <STUDENTS>
      <ID>2456</ID>
      <NAME>Chas Wofford</NAME>
      <SCHOOL>Sam Houston</SCHOOL>
```

```
        <CITY>Houston</CITY>
    </STUDENTS>
    <STUDENTS>
        <ID>3567</ID>
        <NAME>Jerry Kolar</NAME>
        <SCHOOL>Sharpstown</SCHOOL>
        <CITY>Houston</CITY>
    </STUDENTS>
</LIBRARY>

<?xml version="1.0" ?>
<LIBRARY>
    <STUDENTS>
        <ID>1234</ID>
        <NAME>Brad Martin</NAME>
        <SCHOOL>Reagan</SCHOOL>
        <CITY>Austin</CITY>
    </STUDENTS>
    <STUDENTS>
        <ID>2345</ID>
        <NAME>Zac Harvell</NAME>
        <SCHOOL>Westwood</SCHOOL>
        <CITY>Austin</CITY>
    </STUDENTS>
    <STUDENTS>
        <ID>3456</ID>
        <NAME>Walter Smith</NAME>
        <SCHOOL>Bowie</SCHOOL>
        <CITY>Austin</CITY>
    </STUDENTS>
</LIBRARY>
```

First, using the default XML engine behavior, which does not support concatenated XML documents (XMLCONCATENATE=NO), the following SAS program imports the first XML document, which consists of three observations, and produces an error for the second XML document:

```
libname concat xml '/u/My Documents/XML/ConcatStudents.xml';

proc datasets library=concat;
```

Output 3.8 SAS Log Output

```
NOTE: Libref CONCAT was successfully assigned as follows:
      Engine:        XML
      Physical Name: /u/My Documents/XML/ConcatStudents.xml
20   proc datasets library=concat;
ERROR: "xml" is illegal as a processing-instruction target name.
       encountered during XMLMap parsing
       occurred at or near line 23, column 7


                                Directory


      Libref        CONCAT
      Engine        XML
      Physical Name /u/My Documents/XML/ConcatStudents.xml
      XMLType       GENERIC
      XMLMap        NO XMLMAP IN EFFECT



                                            Member
                         #  Name            Type

                         1  STUDENTS  DATA
```

Specifying the LIBNAME statement option XMLCONCATENATE=YES enables the XML engine to import the concatenated XML documents as one SAS data set:

```
libname concat xml '/u/My Documents/XML/ConcatStudents.xml' xmlconcatenate=yes;


proc print data=concat.students;
run;
```

Output 3.9 PROC PRINT Output

```
                        The SAS System                                1

           Obs   CITY      SCHOOL        NAME            ID

            1    Houston   Dellaire      Linda Kay       1345
            2    Houston   Sam Houston   Chas Wofford    2456
            3    Houston   Sharpstown    Jerry Kolar     3567
            4    Austin    Reagan        Brad Martin     1234
            5    Austin    Westwood      Zac Harvell     2345
            6    Austin    Bowie         Walter Smith    3456
```

Importing a CDISC ODM Document

This example imports the XML document that is shown in Appendix 2, "Sample XML Document," on page 129. The document conforms to Version 1.2 of the CDISC Operational Data Model (ODM). To import a CDISC ODM document, you specify **CDISCODM** as the XML format type, and you optionally specify values for the FORMATACTIVE=, FORMATLIBRARY=, and FORMATNOREPLACE= options.

The following SAS program imports the XML document as a SAS data set:

```
filename odm 'C:\Documents and Settings\myid\MyDocuments\CDISC\AE.XML';❶


libname odm xml xmltype=CDISCODM❷ FormatActive=YES❸
   FormatNoReplace=NO❹ FormatLibrary="Work"❺;
```

```
proc print data=odm.AE; ⑥
run;
```

1 The FILENAME statement assigns the fileref ODM to the physical location of the XML document (complete pathname, filename, and file extension).

2 The LIBNAME statement uses the fileref to reference the XML document and specifies the XML engine. By default, the XML engine expects the GENERIC format, so you must include the XMLTYPE= option in order to read the XML document in CDISCODM format.

3 FORMATACTIVE=YES specifies to convert CDISC ODM CodeList elements in the document to SAS formats.

4 FORMATNOREPLACE=NO specifies to replace any existing SAS formats in the format catalog that have the same name as the converted formats.

5 FORMATACTIVE="Work" specifies to create the format catalog in the temporary Work library. The Work library is also the default if you omit the FORMATACTIVE= option.

6 The PRINT procedure produces the output.

Output 3.10 PROC PRINT Output for ODM.AE

```
                              The SAS System                              1

        Obs __STUDYOID

          1 123-456-789
          2 123-456-789

        Obs __METADATAVERSIONOID

          1 v1.1.0
          2 v1.1.0

        Obs __SUBJECTKEY

          1 001
          2 001

        Obs __STUDYEVENTOID

          1 SE.VISIT1
          2 SE.VISIT1

        Obs __FORMOID

          1 FORM.AE
          2 FORM.AE

        Obs __ITEMGROUPOID

          1 IG.AE
          2 IG.AE

        Obs __ITEMGROUPREPEATKEY

          1 1
          2 2

        Obs __TRANSACTIONTYPE

          1 Insert
          2 Insert
                              The SAS System                              2

Obs  TAREA     PNO      SCTRY            F_STATUS              LINE_NO
  1 Oncology  143-02   United States   Source verified, queried      1
  2 Oncology  143-02   United States   Source verified, queried      2

Obs AETERM

  1 HEADACHE
  2 CONGESTION

Obs AESTMON AESTDAY AESTYR AESTDT   AEENMON AEENDAY AEENYR AEENDT   AESEV AEREL

  1  06      10     1999   19990610 06      14      1999   19990614 Mild  None
  2  06      11     1999   19990611                                 Mild  None

Obs

AEOUT                              AEACTTRT   AECONTRT
1 Resolved, no residual effects    None       Medication required
2 Continuing                       None       Medication required
```

The output from PROC CONTENTS displays the file's attributes as well as the attributes of each interpreted column (variable), such as the variable's type and length. The attributes are obtained from the embedded ODM metadata content. The VARNUM option causes the variables to be printed first in alphabetical order and then in the order of their creation.

```
proc contents data=odm.AE varnum;
run;
```

Output 3.11   PROC CONTENTS Output for ODM.AE, Part 1 of 2

```
                        The SAS System                            3

                    The CONTENTS Procedure

            Data Set Name      ODM.AE       Observations         .
            Member Type        DATA         Variables            27
            Engine             XML          Indexes              0
            Created            .            Observation Length   0
            Last Modified      .            Deleted Observations 0
            Protection                      Compressed           NO
            Data Set Type                   Sorted               NO
            Label
            Data Representation  Default
            Encoding             Default


            Alphabetic List of Variables and Attributes

     #  Variable           Type  Len  Format Informat  Label

    26  AEACTTRT           Char   1  $AEACTTR.          Actions taken re studydrug
    27  AECONTRT           Char   1  $AECONTR.          Actions taken, other
    20  AEENDAY            Char   2  $2.        2.      Stop Day-Enter 2 Digits 01-31
    22  AEENDT             Char   8  $8.        $8.     Derived Stop Date
    19  AEENMON            Char   2  $2.        $2.     Stop Month-Enter 2 Digits 01-12
    21  AEENYR             Char   4  $4.        $4.     Stop Year-Enter 4 Digit Year
    25  AEOUT              Char   1  $AEOUT.            Outcome
    24  AEREL              Char   1  $AEREL.            Relationship to study drug
    23  AESEV              Char   1  $AESEV.            Severity
    16  AESTDAY            Char   2  $2.        $2.     Start Day-Enter 2 Digits 01-31
    18  AESTDT             Char   8  $8.        $8.     Derived Start Date
    15  AESTMON            Char   2  $2.        $2.     Start Month-Enter 2 Digits 01-12
    17  AESTYR             Char   4  $4.        $4.     Start Year-Enter 4 Digit Year
    14  AETERM             Char 100  $100.      $100.   Conmed Indication
    12  F_STATUS           Char   1  $F_STATU.          Record status,5 levels,internal use
    13  LINE_NO            Num    8  BEST8.     BEST8.  Line Number
    10  PNO                Char  15  $15.       $15.    Protocol Number
    11  SCTRY              Char   4  $SCTRYF.           Country
     9  TAREA              Char   4  $TAREAF.           Therapeutic Area
     5  __FORMOID          Char 100  $100.      $100.   __FORMOID
     6  __ITEMGROUPOID     Char 100  $100.      $100.   __ITEMGROUPOID
     7  __ITEMGROUPREPEATKEY Char 100  $100.    $100.   __ITEMGROUPREPEATKEY
     2  __METADATAVERSIONOID Char 100  $100.    $100.   __METADATAVERSIONOID
     4  __STUDYEVENTOID    Char 100  $100.      $100.   __STUDYEVENTOID
     1  __STUDYOID         Char 100  $100.      $100.   __STUDYOID
     3  __SUBJECTKEY       Char 100  $100.      $100.   __SUBJECTKEY
     8  __TRANSACTIONTYPE  Char 100  $100.      $100.   __TRANSACTIONTYPE
```

Output 3.12 PROC CONTENTS Output for ODM.AE, Part 2 of 2

```
                    The SAS System                        4

              The CONTENTS Procedure

     Data Set Name      ODM.AE      Observations        .
     Member Type        DATA        Variables           27
     Engine             XML         Indexes             0
     Created            .           Observation Length  0
     Last Modified      .           Deleted Observations 0
     Protection                     Compressed          NO
     Data Set Type                  Sorted              NO
     Label
     Data Representation Default
     Encoding           Default


              Variables in Creation Order

  #  Variable           Type  Len  Format   Informat  Label

  1  __STUDYOID         Char  100  $100.    $100.    __STUDYOID
  2  __METADATAVERSIONOID Char 100 $100.    $100.    __METADATAVERSIONOID
  3  __SUBJECTKEY       Char  100  $100.    $100.    __SUBJECTKEY
  4  __STUDYEVENTOID    Char  100  $100.    $100.    __STUDYEVENTOID
  5  __FORMOID          Char  100  $100.    $100.    __FORMOID
  6  __ITEMGROUPOID     Char  100  $100.    $100.    __ITEMGROUPOID
  7  __ITEMGROUPREPEATKEY Char 100 $100.    $100.    __ITEMGROUPREPEATKEY
  8  __TRANSACTIONTYPE  Char  100  $100.    $100.    __TRANSACTIONTYPE
  9  TAREA              Char    4  $TAREAF.          Therapeutic Area
 10  PNO                Char   15  $15.     $15.     Protocol Number
 11  SCTRY              Char    4  $SCTRYF.          Country
 12  F_STATUS           Char    1  $F_STATU.         Record status, 5 levels, internal use
 13  LINE_NO            Num     8  BEST8.   BEST8.   Line Number
 14  AETERM             Char  100  $100.    $100.    Conmed Indication
 15  AESTMON            Char    2  $2.      $2.      Start Month-Enter 2 Digits 01-12
 16  AESTDAY            Char    2  $2.      $2.      Start Day-Enter 2 Digits 01-31
 17  AESTYR             Char    4  $4.      $4.      Start Year-Enter 4 Digit Year
 18  AESTDT             Char    8  $8.      $8.      Derived Start Date
 19  AEENMON            Char    2  $2.      $2.      Stop Month-Enter 2 Digits 01-12
 20  AEENDAY            Char    2  $2.      $2.      Stop Day-Enter 2 Digits 01-31
 21  AEENYR             Char    4  $4.      $4.      Stop Year-Enter 4 Digit Year
 22  AEENDT             Char    8  $8.      $8.      Derived Stop Date
 23  AESEV              Char    1  $AESEV.           Severity
 24  AEREL              Char    1  $AEREL.           Relationship to study drug
 25  AEOUT              Char    1  $AEOUT.           Outcome
 26  AEACTTRT           Char    1  $AEACTTR.         Actions taken re study drug
 27  AECONTRT           Char    1  $AECONTR.         Actions taken, other
```

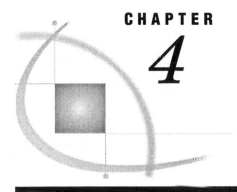

4

Importing XML Documents Using an XMLMap

Why Use an XMLMap When Importing?

The XML engine imports only XML documents that conform to the format types supported in the XMLTYPE= option. Attempting to import free-form XML documents that do not conform to the specifications required by the supported format types will generate errors. To successfully import files that do not conform to the XMLTYPE= format types, you can create a separate XML document, called an XMLMap.

If your XML document does not import successfully, rather than transform the document, you can tell the XML engine how to interpret the XML markup in order to successfully import the XML document. You create a separate XML document, called an *XMLMap*, that contains specific XMLMap syntax, which is XML markup. The XMLMap syntax tells the XML engine how to interpret the XML markup into SAS data set(s), variables (columns), and observations (rows). See Chapter 8, "Creating an XMLMap," on page 95.

After you have created the XMLMap, use the XMLMAP= option either in the LIBNAME statement or as a SAS data set option in order to specify the file.

Understanding the Required Physical Structure for an XML Document to Be Imported Using the GENERIC Format Type

What Is the Required Physical Structure?

For an XML document to be successfully imported, the requirements for well-formed XML must translate as follows:

□ The root-enclosing element (top-level node) of an XML document is the document container. For SAS, it is like the SAS library.

□ The nested elements (repeating element instances) that occur within the container begin with the second-level instance tag.

□ The repeating element instances must represent a rectangular organization. For a SAS data set, they determine the observation boundary that becomes a collection of *rows* with a constant set of *columns*.

Here is an example of an XML document that illustrates the physical structure that is required:

```
<?xml version="1.0" encoding="windows-1252" ?>
<LIBRARY> ❶
   <STUDENTS> ❷
      <ID> 0755 </ID>
      <NAME> Brad Martin </NAME>
      <ADDRESS> 1611 Glengreen </ADDRESS>
      <CITY> Huntsville </CITY>
      <STATE> Texas </STATE>
   </STUDENTS>

   <STUDENTS> ❸
      <ID> 1522 </ID>
      <NAME> Zac Harvell </NAME>
      <ADDRESS> 11900 Glenda </ADDRESS>
      <CITY> Houston </CITY>
      <STATE> Texas </STATE>
   </STUDENTS>
   .
   .  more instances of <STUDENTS>
   .
</LIBRARY>
```

This is what happens when the previous XML document is imported:

1 The XML engine recognizes <LIBRARY> as the root-enclosing element.

2 The engine goes to the second-level instance tag, which is <STUDENTS>, translates it as the data set name, and begins scanning the elements that are nested (contained) between the <STUDENTS> start tag and the </STUDENTS> end tag, looking for variables.

3 Because the instance tags <ID>, <NAME>, <ADDRESS>, <CITY>, and <STATE> are contained within the <STUDENTS> start tag and </STUDENTS> end tag, the XML engine interprets them as variables. The individual instance tag names become the data set variable names. The repeating element instances are translated into a collection of rows with a constant set of columns.

These statements result in the following SAS output:

```
libname test xml 'C:\My Documents\test\students.xml';

proc print data=test.students;
run;
```

Output 4.1 PROC PRINT of TEST.STUDENTS

```
ID        NAME           ADDRESS          CITY           STATE

0755      Brad Martin    1611 Glengreen   Huntsville     Texas
1522      Zac Harvell    11900 Glenda     Houston        Texas
.
.
.
```

Why Is a Specific Physical Structure Required?

Well-formed XML is determined by structure, not content. Therefore, while the XML engine can assume that the XML document is valid, well-formed XML, the engine cannot assume that the root element encloses only instances of a single node element, that is, only a single data set. Therefore, the XML engine has to account for the possibility of multiple nodes, that is, multiple SAS data sets.

For example, when the following correctly structured XML document is imported, it is recognized as containing two SAS data sets: HIGHTEMP and LOWTEMP.

```
<?xml version="1.0" encoding="windows-1252" ?>
<CLIMATE>  ❶
    <HIGHTEMP>  ❷
        <PLACE> Libya </PLACE>
        <DATE> 1922-09-13 </DATE>
        <DEGREE-F> 136 </DEGREE-F>
        <DEGREE-C> 58 </DEGREE-C>
    </HIGHTEMP>
.
.  more instances of <HIGHTEMP>
.
    <LOWTEMP>  ❸
        <PLACE> Antarctica </PLACE>
        <DATE> 1983-07-21 </DATE>
        <DEGREE-F> -129 </DEGREE-F>
        <DEGREE-C> -89 </DEGREE-C>
    </LOWTEMP>
.
.  more instances of <LOWTEMP>
.
</CLIMATE>
```

This is what happens when the previous XML document is imported:

1 The XML engine recognizes the first instance tag <CLIMATE> as the root-enclosing element, which is the container for the document.

2 Starting with the second-level instance tag, which is <HIGHTEMP>, the XML engine uses the repeating element instances as a collection of rows with a constant set of columns.

3 When the second-level instance tag changes, the XML engine interprets that change as a different SAS data set.

The result is two SAS data sets: HIGHTEMP and LOWTEMP. Both happen to have the same variables, but of course, different data.

To ensure that an import result is what you expect, use the DATASETS procedure. For example, these SAS statements result in the following:

```
libname climate xml 'C:\My Documents\xml\climate.xml';


proc datasets library=climate;
quit;
```

Output 4.2   PROC DATASETS Output for CLIMATE Library

```
                    -----Directory-----
        Libref:         CLIMATE
        Engine:         XML
        Physical Name: C:\My Documents\xml\climate.xml

            #  Name       Memtype
            ------------------
            1 HIGHTEMP   DATA
            2 LOWTEMP    DATA
```

Handling XML Documents That Are Not in the Required Physical Structure

If your XML document is not in the required physical structure, you can tell the XML engine how to interpret the XML markup in order to successfully import the document. See Chapter 4, "Importing XML Documents Using an XMLMap," on page 45.

Using an XMLMap to Import an XML Document as One SAS Data Set

This example explains how to create and use an XMLMap in order to tell the XML engine how to map XML markup to a SAS data set, variables, and observations.

First, here is the XML document NHL.XML to be imported. Although simply constructed and relatively easy for you to read, it does not import successfully because its XML markup is not in the required physical structure:

```
<?xml version="1.0" encoding="iso-8859-1" ?>
<NHL>
  <CONFERENCE> Eastern
    <DIVISION> Southeast
      <TEAM name="Thrashers"  abbrev="ATL" />
      <TEAM name="Hurricanes" abbrev="CAR" />
      <TEAM name="Panthers"   abbrev="FLA" />
      <TEAM name="Lightning"  abbrev="TB" />
      <TEAM name="Capitals"   abbrev="WSH" />
    </DIVISION>
  </CONFERENCE>

  <CONFERENCE> Western
    <DIVISION> Pacific
      <TEAM name="Stars"    abbrev="DAL" />
      <TEAM name="Kings"    abbrev="LA" />
      <TEAM name="Ducks"    abbrev="ANA" />
```

```
      <TEAM name="Coyotes" abbrev="PHX" />
      <TEAM name="Sharks"  abbrev="SJ" />
    </DIVISION>
   </CONFERENCE>
 </NHL>
```

To successfully import the XML document, an XMLMap is needed. After familiarizing yourself with the data to be imported, you can code the XMLMap syntax so that the data is successfully imported. Here is the XMLMap used to import the XML document, with notations as to the data investigation:

```
<?xml version="1.0" ?>
<SXLEMAP version="1.2">
  <TABLE name="TEAMS"> ❶
        <TABLE-PATH syntax="xpath"> ❷
           /NHL/CONFERENCE/DIVISION/TEAM
         </TABLE-PATH>

        <COLUMN name="name"> ❸
          <PATH> ❺
             /NHL/CONFERENCE/DIVISION/TEAM/@name
            </PATH>
            <TYPE>character</TYPE>
            <DATATYPE>STRING</DATATYPE>
            <LENGTH>30</LENGTH>
          </COLUMN>

        <COLUMN name="abbrev"> ❸
          <PATH> ❺
           /NHL/CONFERENCE/DIVISION/TEAM/@abbrev
            </PATH>
            <TYPE>character</TYPE>
            <DATATYPE>STRING</DATATYPE>
            <LENGTH>3</LENGTH>
          </COLUMN>

        <COLUMN name="CONFERENCE" retain="YES"> ❹
           <PATH>/NHL/CONFERENCE</PATH> ❺
            <TYPE>character</TYPE>
            <DATATYPE>STRING</DATATYPE>
            <LENGTH>10</LENGTH>
          </COLUMN>

        <COLUMN name="DIVISION" retain="YES"> ❹
           <PATH> ❺
              /NHL/CONFERENCE/DIVISION
            </PATH>
            <TYPE>character</TYPE>
            <DATATYPE>STRING</DATATYPE>
            <LENGTH>10</LENGTH>
          </COLUMN>
    </TABLE>
  </SXLEMAP>
```

The previous XMLMap syntax defines how to translate the XML markup as explained below, using the following data investigation steps:

1 *Locate and identify distinct tables of information.*

   You want a SAS data set (table) that contains some of the teams of the National Hockey League. Because that is the only information contained in the XML document, you can define a single data set named TEAMS in the XMLMap. (Note that other XML documents might contain more than one table of related information. Importing multiple tables is supported by the XMLMap syntax as shown in "Using an XMLMap to Import an XML Document as Multiple SAS Data Sets" on page 51.)

2 *Identify the SAS data set observation boundary, which translates into a collection of rows with a constant set of columns.*

   In the XML document, information about individual teams occurs in a <TEAM> tag located with <CONFERENCE> and <DIVISION> enclosures. You want a new observation generated each time a TEAM element is read.

3 *Collect column definitions for each table.*

   For this XML document, the data content form is mixed. Some data occurs as XML PCDATA (for example, CONFERENCE), and other data is contained in attribute-value pairs (for example, NAME). Data types are all string values. The constructed observation will also include the team NAME and ABBREV. A length of 30 characters is sufficient for the NAME, and three characters is enough for the ABBREV field contents.

4 *Add foreign keys or required external context.*

   You want to include information about the league orientation for the teams. Also, you want to extract CONFERENCE and DIVISION data.

   Note: The retain= attribute in the column definition forces retention of processed data values after an observation is written to the output data set. Because the foreign key fields occur outside the observation boundary (that is, they are more sparsely populated in the hierarchical XML data than in the SAS observation), their values for additional rows need to be retained as they are encountered. △

5 *Define a location path for each variable definition.*

   The PATH element identifies a position in the XML document from which to extract data for each column. Element-parsed character data is treated differently than attribute values. There is no conditional selection criteria involved.

The following SAS statements import the XML document NHL.XML and specify the XMLMap named NHL.MAP. The PRINT procedure verifies that the import is successful:

```
filename NHL 'C:\My Documents\XML\NHL.xml';
filename MAP 'C:\My Documents\XML\NHL.map';
libname NHL xml xmlmap=MAP;

proc print data=NHL.TEAMS noobs;
run;
```

Output 4.3   PROC PRINT of Data Set NHL.TEAMS

```
                                      The SAS System

             name                        abbrev    CONFERENCE    DIVISION

             Thrashers                    ATL       Eastern       Southeast
             Hurricanes                   CAR       Eastern       Southeast
             Panthers                     FLA       Eastern       Southeast
             Lightning                    TB        Eastern       Southeast
             Capitals                     WSH       Eastern       Southeast
             Stars                        DAL       Western       Pacific
             Kings                        LA        Western       Pacific
             Ducks                        ANA       Western       Pacific
             Coyotes                      PHX       Western       Pacific
             Sharks                       SJ        Western       Pacific
```

Using an XMLMap to Import an XML Document as Multiple SAS Data Sets

This example explains how to create and use an XMLMap in order to define how to map XML markup into two SAS data sets. The example uses the XML document RSS.XML, which does not import successfully because its XML markup is incorrectly structured for the XML engine to translate successfully.

Note: The XML document RSS.XML uses the XML format RSS (Rich Site Summary), which was designed by Netscape originally for exchange of content within the My Netscape Network (MNN) community. The RSS format has been widely adopted for sharing headlines and other Web content and is a good example of XML as a transmission format. △

First, here is the XML document RSS.XML to be imported:

```
<?xml version="1.0" encoding="ISO-8859-1" ?>
<rss version="0.91">
   <channel>
      <title>WriteTheWeb</title>
<link>http://writetheweb.com</link>
      <description>News for web users that write back</description>
      <language>en-us</language>
      <copyright>Copyright 2000, WriteTheWeb team.</copyright>
      <managingEditor>editor@writetheweb.com</managingEditor>
      <webMaster>webmaster@writetheweb.com</webMaster>
      <image>
         <title>WriteTheWeb</title>
<url>http://writetheweb.com/images/mynetscape88.gif</url>
<link>http://writetheweb.com</link>
<width>88</width>
<height>31</height>
<description>News for web users that write back</description>
</image>
      <item>
         <title>Giving the world a pluggable Gnutella</title>
<link>http://writetheweb.com/read.php?item=24</link>
      <description>WorldOS is a framework on which to build programs that work
like Freenet or Gnutella -allowing distributed applications using
```

```
peer-to-peer routing.</description>
      </item>
      <item>
          <title>Syndication discussions hot up</title>
    <link>http://writetheweb.com/read.php?item=23</link>
    <description>After a period of dormancy, the Syndication mailing list
has become active again, with contributions from leaders in traditional media
and Web syndication.</description>
      </item>
    <item>
          <title>Personal web server integrates file sharing and messaging
    </title>
    <link>http://writetheweb.com/read.php?item=22</link>
    <description>The Magi Project is an innovative project to create a
combined personal web server and messaging system that enables the sharing
and synchronization of information across desktop, laptop and palmtop devices.
      </description>
      </item>
      <item>
          <title>Syndication and Metadata</title>
    <link>http://writetheweb.com/read.php?item=21</link>
    <description>RSS is probably the best known metadata format around.
RDF is probably one of the least understood. In this essay, published on my
O&apos;Reilly Network weblog, I argue that the next generation of RSS
should be based on RDF.</description>
      </item>
      <item>
          <title>UK bloggers get organized</title>
    <link>http://writetheweb.com/read.php?item=20</link>
    <description>Looks like the weblogs scene is gathering pace beyond
the shores of the US. There&apos;s now a UK-specific page on weblogs.com,
and a mailing list at egroups.</description>
      </item>
      <item>
          <title>Yournamehere.com more important than anything</title>
    <link>http://writetheweb.com/read.php?item=19</link>
    <description>Whatever you&apos;re publishing on the web, your site
name is the most valuable asset you have, according to Carl Steadman.
      </description>
      </item>
    </channel>
  </rss>
```

The XML document can be successfully imported by creating an XMLMap that
defines how to map the XML markup. The following is the XMLMap named RSS.MAP,
which contains the syntax that is needed to successfully import RSS.XML. The syntax
tells the XML engine how to interpret the XML markup as explained in the subsequent
descriptions. Note that the contents of RSS.XML will result in two SAS data sets:
CHANNEL to contain content information and ITEMS to contain the individual news
stories.

```
<?xml version="1.0" ?>

<SXLEMAP version="1.2"> ❶
```

```
<!-- TABLE (CHANNEL) -->
<!-- top level channel content description (TOC) -->
<TABLE name="CHANNEL"> ❷
   <TABLE-PATH syntax="xpath"> /rss/channel </TABLE-PATH> ❸
   <TABLE-END-PATH syntax="xpath" beginend="Begin">
      /rss/channel/item </TABLE-END-PATH> ❹

   <!-- title -->
   <COLUMN name="title"> ❺
      <PATH> /rss/channel/title </PATH>
      <TYPE> character </TYPE>
      <DATATYPE> string </DATATYPE>
      <LENGTH> 200 </LENGTH>
   </COLUMN>

   <!-- link -->
   <COLUMN name="link"> ❻
      <PATH> /rss/channel/link </PATH>
      <TYPE> character </TYPE>
      <DATATYPE> string </DATATYPE>
      <LENGTH> 200 </LENGTH>
      <DESCRIPTION> Story link </DESCRIPTION>
   </COLUMN>

   <!-- description -->
   <COLUMN name="description">
      <PATH> /rss/channel/description </PATH>
      <TYPE> character </TYPE>
      <DATATYPE> string </DATATYPE>
      <LENGTH> 1024 </LENGTH>
   </COLUMN>

   <!-- language -->
   <COLUMN name="language">
      <PATH> /rss/channel/language </PATH>
      <TYPE> character </TYPE>
      <DATATYPE> string </DATATYPE>
      <LENGTH> 8 </LENGTH>
   </COLUMN>

   <!-- version -->
   <COLUMN name="version"> ❼
      <PATH> /rss@version </PATH>
      <TYPE> character </TYPE>
      <DATATYPE> string </DATATYPE>
      <LENGTH> 8 </LENGTH>
   </COLUMN>
</TABLE>


<!-- TABLE (ITEMS) -->
<!-- individual news stories -->
<TABLE name="ITEMS"> ❽
   <TABLE-PATH syntax="xpath"> /rss/channel/item </TABLE-PATH>
```

```
          <TABLE-DESCRIPTION> Individual news stories </TABLE-DESCRIPTION>

          <!-- title -->
          <COLUMN name="title"> ❾
             <PATH> /rss/channel/item/title </PATH>
             <TYPE> character </TYPE>
             <DATATYPE> string </DATATYPE>
             <LENGTH> 200 </LENGTH>
          </COLUMN>

          <!-- link -->
          <!-- link is renamed to url, assigned a label and max length -->
          <COLUMN name="URL"> ❿
             <PATH> /rss/channel/item/link </PATH>
             <TYPE> character </TYPE>
             <DATATYPE> string </DATATYPE>
             <LENGTH> 200 </LENGTH>
             <DESCRIPTION> Story link </DESCRIPTION>
          </COLUMN>

          <!-- description -->
          <COLUMN name="description">
             <PATH> /rss/channel/item/description </PATH>
             <TYPE> character </TYPE>
             <DATATYPE> string </DATATYPE>
             <LENGTH> 1024 </LENGTH>
          </COLUMN>
       </TABLE>

</SXLEMap>
```

The previous XMLMap defines how to translate the XML markup as explained below:

1 Root-enclosing element for SAS data set definitions.

2 Element for the CHANNEL data set definition.

3 Element specifying the location path that defines where in the XML document to collect variables for the CHANNEL data set.

4 Element specifying the location path that specifies when to stop processing data for the CHANNEL data set.

5 Element containing the attributes for the TITLE variable in the CHANNEL data set. The XPath construction specifies where to find the current tag and to access data from the named element.

6 Subsequent COLUMN elements define the variables LINK, DESCRIPTION, and LANGUAGE for the CHANNEL data set.

7 Element containing the attributes for the last variable in the CHANNEL data set, which is VERSION. This XPath construction specifies where to find the current tag and uses the attribute form to access data from the named attribute.

8 Element for the ITEMS data set definition.

9 Element containing the attributes for the TITLE variable in the ITEMS data set.

10 Subsequent COLUMN elements define other variables for the ITEMS data set, which are URL and DESCRIPTION.

The following SAS statements import the XML document RSS.XML and specify the XMLMap named RSS.MAP. The DATASETS procedure then verifies the import results:

```
filename rss 'C:\My Documents\xml\rss.xml';
filename map 'C:\My Documents\xml\rss.map';

libname rss xml xmlmap=map access=readonly;

proc datasets library=rss;
run;
quit;
```

Output 4.4   PROC DATASETS Output for RSS Library Showing Two Data Sets

```
                       -----Directory-----

              Libref:        RSS
              Engine:        XML
              Physical Name: C:\My Documents\xml\rss.xml
              XMLType:       GENERIC
              XMLMap:        MAP


              #  Name      Memtype
              -------------------
              1  CHANNEL   DATA
              2  ITEMS     DATA
```

Importing Hierarchical Data as Related Data Sets

XML documents often contain hierarchical data in that the data is structured into different levels like a company organization chart. Hierarchical structures are one-to-many relationships, with top items having one or more items below it, for example, customer to orders.

This example explains how to define an XMLMap in order to import an XML document as two data sets that have related information.

First, here is the XML document Pharmacy.XML. The file contains hierarchical data with related entities in the form of individual customers and their prescriptions. Each customer can have one or multiple prescriptions. Notice that PRESCRIPTION elements are nested within each <PERSON> start tag and </PERSON> end tag:

```
<?xml version="1.0" ?>
<PHARMACY>
  <PERSON>
    <NAME>Brad Martin</NAME>
    <STREET>11900 Glenda Court</STREET>
    <CITY>Austin</CITY>
   <PRESCRIPTION>
    <NUMBER>1234</NUMBER>
    <DRUG>Tetracycline</DRUG>
  </PRESCRIPTION>
  <PRESCRIPTION>
    <NUMBER>1245</NUMBER>
    <DRUG>Lomotil</DRUG>
  </PRESCRIPTION>
```

```
    </PERSON>
  <PERSON>
    <NAME>Jim Spano</NAME>
    <STREET>1611 Glengreen</STREET>
    <CITY>Austin</CITY>
  <PRESCRIPTION>
    <NUMBER>1268</NUMBER>
    <DRUG>Nexium</DRUG>
  </PRESCRIPTION>
  </PERSON>
</PHARMACY>
```

To import separate data sets, one describing the customers and the other containing prescription information, a relation between each customer and associated prescriptions must be designated in order to know which prescriptions belong to each customer.

An XMLMap defines how to translate the XML markup into two SAS data sets. The customer table imports the name and address of each customer, and the prescription table imports the customer's name, prescription number, and drug. Notations in the XMLMap syntax are explained below.

Note: The XMLMap was generated by using SAS XML Mapper. △

```
<?xml version="1.0" encoding="UTF-8"?>

<!-- ############################################################ -->
<!-- 2003-04-08T15:03:16 -->
<!-- SAS XML Libname Engine Map -->
<!-- Generated by XML Mapper, 9.1.10.20030407.1378 -->
<!-- ############################################################ -->

<SXLEMAP version="1.2" name="SXLEMAP"> ❶

  <!-- ############################################################ -->
  <TABLE name="PERSON"> ❷
    <TABLE-PATH syntax="XPath">/PHARMACY/PERSON</TABLE-PATH>

    <COLUMN name="NAME"> ❸
      <PATH  syntax="XPath">/PHARMACY/PERSON/NAME</PATH>
      <TYPE>character</TYPE>
      <DATATYPE>string</DATATYPE>
      <LENGTH>11</LENGTH>
    </COLUMN>

    <COLUMN name="STREET"> ❸
      <PATH  syntax="XPath">/PHARMACY/PERSON/STREET</PATH>
      <TYPE>character</TYPE>
      <DATATYPE>string</DATATYPE>
      <LENGTH>18</LENGTH>
    </COLUMN>

    <COLUMN name="CITY"> ❸
      <PATH  syntax="XPath">/PHARMACY/PERSON/CITY</PATH>
      <TYPE>character</TYPE>
      <DATATYPE>string</DATATYPE>
```

```
        <LENGTH>6</LENGTH>
      </COLUMN>

  </TABLE>

  <!-- ############################################################# -->
  <TABLE name="PRESCRIPTION"> ❹
    <TABLE-PATH syntax="XPath">/PHARMACY/PERSON/PRESCRIPTION</TABLE-PATH>

    <COLUMN name="NAME" retain="YES"> ❺
      <PATH   syntax="XPath">/PHARMACY/PERSON/NAME</PATH>
      <TYPE>character</TYPE>
      <DATATYPE>string</DATATYPE>
      <LENGTH>11</LENGTH>
    </COLUMN>

    <COLUMN name="NUMBER"> ❻
      <PATH   syntax="XPath">/PHARMACY/PERSON/PRESCRIPTION/NUMBER</PATH>
      <TYPE>numeric</TYPE>
      <DATATYPE>integer</DATATYPE>
    </COLUMN>

    <COLUMN name="DRUG"> ❻
      <PATH   syntax="XPath">/PHARMACY/PERSON/PRESCRIPTION/DRUG</PATH>
      <TYPE>character</TYPE>
      <DATATYPE>string</DATATYPE>
      <LENGTH>12</LENGTH>
    </COLUMN>

  </TABLE>

</SXLEMAP>
```

1 SXLEMAP is the root-enclosing element for the two SAS data set definitions.

2 First TABLE element defines the Person data set.

3 COLUMN elements contain the attributes for the Name, Street, and City variables in the Person data set.

4 Second TABLE element defines the Prescription data set.

5 COLUMN element contains the attributes for the Name variable in the Prescription data set. Specifying the **retain="yes"** attribute causes the name to be held for each observation until it is replaced by a different value. (Note that this is much like using the SAS DATA step RETAIN statement, which causes a variable to retain its value from one iteration of the DATA step to the next.)

6 COLUMN elements contain the attributes for the Number and Drug variables in the Prescription data set.

The following SAS statements import the XML document and specify the XMLMap:

```
filename pharm 'c:\My Documents\XML\Pharmacy.xml';
filename map 'c:\My Documents\XML\Pharmacy.map';
libname pharm xml xmlmap=map;
```

The DATASETS procedure verifies that SAS interprets the XML document Pharmacy.XML as two SAS data sets: PHARM.PERSON and PHARM.PRESCRIPTION.

```
proc datasets library=pharm;
```

Output 4.5   PROC DATASETS Output for the PHARM Data Library

```
5      proc datasets library=pharm;
                                          Directory

                                Libref        PHARM
                                Engine        XML
                                Physical Name PHARM
                                XMLType       GENERIC
                                XMLMap        MAP


                                              Member
                            #  Name           Type

                            1  PERSON         DATA
                            2  PRESCRIPTION   DATA
```

Here is PROC PRINT output for both of the imported SAS data sets.

Output 4.6   PROC PRINT Output for PHARM.PERSON

```
                        The SAS System                    1

        Obs    NAME              STREET              CITY

         1     Brad Martin       11900 Glenda Court  Austin
         2     Jim Spano         1611 Glengreen      Austin
```

Output 4.7   PROC PRINT Output for PHARM.PRESCRIPTION

```
                        The SAS System                    2

        Obs    NAME              NUMBER    DRUG

         1     Brad Martin       1234      Tetracycline
         2     Brad Martin       1245      Lomotil
         3     Jim Spano         1268      Nexium
```

Including a Key Field with Generated Numeric Keys

This example imports the XML document Pharmacy.XML, which contains hierarchical data and is used in the example "Importing Hierarchical Data as Related Data Sets" on page 55. This example continues with the XMLMap by adding a key field with generated numeric key values in order to provide a relationship between the two data sets. (A key field holds unique data in order to identify that record from the other records. For example, account number, product code, and customer name are typical key fields.)

To generate key field values, use the **ordinal="yes"** attribute in the COLUMN element in order to create a counter variable. A counter variable keeps track of the number of times the location path, which is specified by the INCREMENT-PATH element, is encountered. The counter variable increments its count by 1 each time the path is matched. (The counter variable is similar to the _N_ automatic variable in DATA step processing in that it counts the number of observations being read into a SAS data set.)

Note: When using a counter variable to create a key field for related data sets, you must specify the same location paths for both TABLE elements; otherwise, the results will not match. Each table must have the same generated key for like-named data elements. △

The following XMLMap imports Pharmacy.XML document as two SAS data sets that have related information and also creates a key field that holds generated numeric key values:

```
<?xml version="1.0" encoding="UTF-8" ?>

<!-- ######################################################## -->
<!-- 2003-04-15T10:55:43 -->
<!-- SAS XML Libname Engine Map -->
<!-- Generated by XML Mapper, 9.1.10.20030413.1400 -->
<!-- ######################################################## -->

<SXLEMAP version="1.2" name="SXLEMAP">

  <!-- ######################################################## -->
  <TABLE name="PERSON">
    <TABLE-PATH syntax="XPath">/PHARMACY/PERSON</TABLE-PATH> ❶

    <COLUMN name="KEY" retain="YES" ordinal="YES"> ❷
      <INCREMENT-PATH syntax="XPath">/PHARMACY/PERSON</INCREMENT-PATH>
      <TYPE>numeric</TYPE>
      <DATATYPE>integer</DATATYPE>
      <FORMAT width="3">Z</FORMAT>
    </COLUMN>

    <COLUMN name="NAME">
      <PATH    syntax="XPath">/PHARMACY/PERSON/NAME</PATH>
      <TYPE>character</TYPE>
      <DATATYPE>string</DATATYPE>
      <LENGTH>11</LENGTH>
    </COLUMN>

    <COLUMN name="STREET">
      <PATH    syntax="XPath">/PHARMACY/PERSON/STREET</PATH>
      <TYPE>character</TYPE>
      <DATATYPE>string</DATATYPE>
      <LENGTH>18</LENGTH>
    </COLUMN>

    <COLUMN name="CITY">
      <PATH    syntax="XPath">/PHARMACY/PERSON/CITY</PATH>
      <TYPE>character</TYPE>
      <DATATYPE>string</DATATYPE>
      <LENGTH>6</LENGTH>
    </COLUMN>
```

```
    </TABLE>

    <!-- ############################################################# -->
    <TABLE name="PRESCRIPTION">
      <TABLE-PATH syntax="XPath">/PHARMACY/PERSON/PRESCRIPTION</TABLE-PATH> ❸

      <COLUMN name="KEY" retain="YES" ordinal="YES"> ❹
        <INCREMENT-PATH syntax="XPath">/PHARMACY/PERSON</INCREMENT-PATH>
        <TYPE>numeric</TYPE>
        <DATATYPE>integer</DATATYPE>
        <FORMAT width="3">Z</FORMAT>
      </COLUMN>

      <COLUMN name="NUMBER">
        <PATH  syntax="XPath">/PHARMACY/PERSON/PRESCRIPTION/NUMBER</PATH>
        <TYPE>numeric</TYPE>
        <DATATYPE>integer</DATATYPE>
      </COLUMN>

      <COLUMN name="DRUG">
        <PATH  syntax="XPath">/PHARMACY/PERSON/PRESCRIPTION/DRUG</PATH>
        <TYPE>character</TYPE>
        <DATATYPE>string</DATATYPE>
        <LENGTH>12</LENGTH>
      </COLUMN>

    </TABLE>

</SXLEMAP>
```

The following explains the XMLMap syntax that generates the key fields:

1 In the TABLE element that defines the Person data set, the TABLE-PATH element identifies the observation boundary for the data set. The location path generates a new observation each time a PERSON element is read.

2 For the Person data set, the COLUMN element for the Key variable contains the **ordinal="yes"** attribute as well as the INCREMENT-PATH element. This is the process that the XML engine follows in order to generate the key field values for the Person data set:

   a When the XML engine encounters the <PERSON> start tag, it reads the value into the input buffer, then increments the value for the Key variable by 1.

   b The XML engine continues reading values into the input buffer until it encounters the </PERSON> end tag, at which time it writes the completed input buffer to the SAS data set as one observation.

   c The process is repeated for each <PERSON> start tag (from INCREMENT-PATH) and </PERSON> end tag (from TABLE-PATH) sequence.

   d The result is four variables and two observations.

3 In the TABLE element that defines the Prescription data set, the TABLE-PATH element identifies the observation boundary for the data set. The location path generates a new observation each time a PRESCRIPTION element is read.

4 For the Prescription data set, the COLUMN element for the Key variable contains the **ordinal="yes"** attribute as well as the INCREMENT-PATH element.

This is the process that the XML engine follows in order to generate the key field values for the Prescription data set:

a   When the XML engine encounters the <PERSON> start tag, it reads the value into the input buffer, then increments the value for the Key variable by 1.

b   The XML engine continues reading values into the input buffer until it encounters the </PRESCRIPTION> end tag, at which time it writes the completed input buffer to the SAS data set as one observation.

> *Note:*   Because the increment paths for the counter variables must be the same for both TABLE elements, the behavior of the XML engine for the Prescription table Key variable is the same as the Person table Key variable. While the XML engine tracks the occurrence of a PERSON tag as a key for both counter variables, the observations are derived from different TABLE-PATH locations. △

c   The process is repeated for each <PERSON> start tag (from INCREMENT-PATH) and </PRESCRIPTION> end tag (from TABLE-PATH) sequence.

d   The result is three variables and three observations.

The following SAS statements import the XML document:

```
filename pharm 'c:\My Documents\XML\Pharmacy.xml';
filename map 'c:\My Documents\XML\PharmacyOrdinal.map';
libname pharm xml xmlmap=map;
```

Here is PROC PRINT output for both of the imported SAS data sets with a numeric key:

Output 4.8   PROC PRINT Output for PHARM.PERSON

```
                    The SAS System                                      1

    Obs        KEY    NAME          STREET              CITY

     1         001    Brad Martin   11900 Glenda Court  Austin
     2         002    Jim Spano     1611 Glengreen      Austin
```

Output 4.9   PROC PRINT Output for PHARM.PRESCRIPTION

```
                    The SAS System                                      2

    Obs          KEY      NUMBER    DRUG

     1           001      1234      Tetracycline
     2           001      1245      Lomotil
     3           002      1268      Nexium
```

Determining the Observation Boundary to Avoid Concatenated Data

This example imports an XML document that illustrates how to determine the observation boundary so that the result is separate observations and not concatenated data.

The observation boundary translates into a collection of rows with a constant set of columns. Using an XMLMap, you determine the observation boundary with the TABLE-PATH element by specifying a location path. The end tag for the location path determines when data is written to the SAS data set as an observation.

Identifying the observation boundary can be tricky due to sequences of start tag and end-tag pairing. If you do not identify the appropriate observation boundary, the result could be a concatenated data string instead of separate observations. This example illustrates pairing situations that can cause unwanted results.

For the following XML document, an XMLMap is necessary in order to import the file successfully. Without an XMLMap, the XML engine would import a data set named FORD with columns ROW0, MODEL0, YEAR0, ROW1, MODEL1, YEAR1, and so on.

```
<?xml version="1.0" ?>
<VEHICLES>
  <FORD>
    <ROW>
      <Model>Mustang</Model>
      <Year>1965</Year>
    </ROW>
    <ROW>
      <Model>Explorer</Model>
      <Year>1982</Year>
    </ROW>
    <ROW>
      <Model>Taurus</Model>
      <Year>1998</Year>
    </ROW>
    <ROW>
      <Model>F150</Model>
      <Year>2000</Year>
    </ROW>
  </FORD>
</VEHICLES>
```

Looking at the above XML document, there are three sequences of element start tags and end tags: VEHICLES, FORD, and ROW. If you specify the following table location path and column locations paths, this is the process that the XML engine would follow:

```
<TABLE-PATH syntax="xpath"> /VEHICLES/FORD </TABLE-PATH>
  <PATH syntax="xpath"> /VEHICLES/FORD/ROW/Model </PATH>
  <PATH syntax="xpath"> /VEHICLES/FORD/ROW/Year </PATH>
```

1 The XML engine reads the XML markup until it encounters the <FORD> start tag, because FORD is the last element specified in the table location path.

2 The XML engine clears the input buffer and scans subsequent elements for variables based on the column location paths. As a value for each variable is encountered, it is read into the input buffer. For example, after reading the first ROW element, the input buffer contains the values **Mustang** and **1965**.

3 The XML engine continues reading values into the input buffer until it encounters the </FORD> end tag, at which time it writes the completed input buffer to the SAS data set as an observation.

4 The end result is one observation, which is not what you want.

Here is PROC PRINT output showing the concatenated observation. (Note that the data in the observation is truncated due to the LENGTH element.)

Output 4.10 PROC PRINT Output Showing Unacceptable FORD Data Set

```
                              The SAS System                              1

                        Model                Year

                        Mustang Explorer Tau  1965
```

To get separate observations, you must change the table location path so that the XML engine writes separate observations to the SAS data set. Here are the correct location paths and the process that the engine would follow:

```
<TABLE-PATH syntax="xpath"> /VEHICLES/FORD/ROW </TABLE-PATH>
  <PATH syntax="xpath"> /VEHICLES/FORD/ROW/Model </PATH>
  <PATH syntax="xpath"> /VEHICLES/FORD/ROW/Year </PATH>
```

1 The XML engine reads the XML markup until it encounters the <ROW> start tag, because ROW is the last element specified in the table location path.

2 The XML engine clears the input buffer and scans subsequent elements for variables based on the column location paths. As a value for each variable is encountered, it is read into the input buffer.

3 The XML engine continues reading values into the input buffer until it encounters the </ROW> end tag, at which time it writes the completed input buffer to the SAS data set as an observation. That is, one observation is written to the SAS data set that contains the values **Mustang** and **1965**.

4 The process is repeated for each <ROW> start-tag and </ROW> end-tag sequence.

5 The result is four observations.

Here is the complete XMLMap syntax:

```
<?xml version="1.0" ?>
<SXLEMAP version="1.2" name="path" description="XMLMap for path">
  <TABLE name="FORD">
    <TABLE-PATH syntax="xpath"> /VEHICLES/FORD/ROW </TABLE-PATH>
    <COLUMN name="Model">
      <DATATYPE> string </DATATYPE>
      <LENGTH> 20 </LENGTH>
      <TYPE> character </TYPE>
      <PATH syntax="xpath"> /VEHICLES/FORD/ROW/Model </PATH>
    </COLUMN>
    <COLUMN name="Year">
      <DATATYPE> string </DATATYPE>
      <LENGTH> 4 </LENGTH>
      <TYPE> character </TYPE>
      <PATH syntax="xpath"> /VEHICLES/FORD/ROW/Year </PATH>
    </COLUMN>
  </TABLE>
</SXLEMAP>
```

The following SAS statements import the XML document and specify the XMLMap. The PRINT procedure verifies the results.

```
filename PATH 'c:\My Documents\XML\path.xml';
filename MAP 'c:\My Documents\XML\path.map';
libname PATH xml xmlmap=MAP;
```

```
proc print data=PATH.FORD noobs;
run;
```

Output 4.11   PROC PRINT Output Showing Desired FORD Data Set

```
                              The SAS System                                1

                    Model                    Year

                    Mustang                  1965
                    Explorer                 1982
                    Taurus                   1998
                    F150                     2000
```

Determining the Observation Boundary to Select the Best Columns

This example imports an XML document that illustrates how to determine the observation boundary so that the result is the best collection of columns.

The observation boundary translates into a collection of rows with a constant set of columns. Using an XMLMap, you determine the observation boundary with the TABLE-PATH element by specifying a location path.

In the following XML document, PUBLICATION appears to be a possible element to use as the observation boundary, which would result in these columns: TITLE, ACQUIRED, TOPIC. However, the TOPIC element occurs arbitrarily within a single PUBLICATION container, so the result would be a set of columns with TOPIC occurring more than once. Therefore, the TOPIC element is the better choice to use as the observation boundary in order to result in these columns: TITLE, ACQUIRED, TOPIC, MAJOR.

```xml
<?xml version="1.0" encoding="iso-8859-1" ?>
<Library>
  <Publication>
    <Title>Developer's Almanac</Title>
    <Acquired>12-11-2000</Acquired>
    <Topic Major="Y">JAVA</Topic>
  </Publication>
  <Publication>
    <Title>Inside Visual C++</Title>
    <Acquired>06-19-1998</Acquired>
    <Topic>Major="Y">C</Topic>
    <Topic>Reference</Topic>
  </Publication>
  <Publication>
    <Title>Core Servlets</Title>
    <Acquired>05-30-2001</Acquired>
    <Topic Major="Y">JAVA</Topic>
    <Topic>Servlets</Topic>
    <Topic>Reference</Topic>
  </Publication>
</Library>
```

Here is the XMLMap syntax to use in order to import the previous XML document:

```
<?xml version="1.0" ?>
<SXLEMAP version="1.2">
  <TABLE name="Publication">
    <TABLE-PATH syntax="xpath">
        /Library/Publication/Topic ❶
    </TABLE-PATH>

    <COLUMN name="Title" retain="YES">
      <PATH>
          /Library/Publication/Title
      </PATH>
      <TYPE>character</TYPE>
      <DATATYPE>STRING</DATATYPE>
      <LENGTH>19</LENGTH>
    </COLUMN>

    <COLUMN name="Acquired" retain="YES">
      <PATH>
         /Library/Publication/Acquired
      </PATH>
      <TYPE>numeric</TYPE>
      <DATATYPE>FLOAT</DATATYPE>
      <LENGTH>10</LENGTH>
      <FORMAT width="10" >mmddyy</FORMAT> ❷
      <INFORMAT width="10" >mmddyy</INFORMAT>
    </COLUMN>

    <COLUMN name="Topic">
      <PATH>
          /Library/Publication/Topic</PATH>
      <TYPE>character</TYPE>
      <DATATYPE>STRING</DATATYPE>
      <LENGTH>9</LENGTH>
    </COLUMN>

    <COLUMN name="Major">
      <PATH>
          /Library/Publication/Topic/@Major
      </PATH>
      <TYPE>character</TYPE>
      <DATATYPE>STRING</DATATYPE>
      <LENGTH>1</LENGTH>
      <ENUM> ❸
        <VALUE>Y</VALUE>
        <VALUE>N</VALUE>
      </ENUM>
     <DEFAULT>N</DEFAULT> ❹
    </COLUMN>
  </TABLE>
</SXLEMAP>
```

The previous XMLMap tells the XML engine how to interpret the XML markup as explained below:

1   The TOPIC element determines the location path that defines where in the XML document to collect variables for the SAS data set. An observation is written each time a </TOPIC> end tag is encountered in the XML document.

2   For the ACQUIRED column, the date is constructed using the XMLMap syntax FORMAT element. Elements like FORMAT and INFORMAT are useful for situations where data must be converted for use by SAS. The XML engine also supports user-written formats and informats, which can be used independently of each other.

3   Enumerations are also supported by XMLMap syntax. The ENUM element specifies that the values for the column MAJOR must be either Y or N. Incoming values not contained within the ENUM list are set to MISSING.

4   By default, a missing value is set to MISSING. The DEFAULT element specifies a default value for a missing value, which for this example is specified as N. Note that when the ENUM element is used, a value specified by DEFAULT must be one of the ENUM values in order to be valid.

The following SAS statements import the XML document and specify the XMLMap. The PRINT procedure verifies the results.

```
filename REP 'C:\My Documents\XML\Rep.xml';
filename MAP 'C:\My Documents\XML\Rep.map';
libname REP xml xmlmap=MAP;

proc print data=REP.Publication noobs;
run;
```

Output 4.12   PROC PRINT Output for PUBLICATION Data Set

```
                          The SAS System                              1

            Title                 Acquired    Topic       Major

            Developer's Almanac    12/11/2000  JAVA         Y
            Inside Visual C++      06/19/1998  C            Y
            Inside Visual C++      06/19/1998  Reference    N
            Core Servlets          05/30/2001  JAVA         Y
            Core Servlets          05/30/2001  Servlets     N
            Core Servlets          05/30/2001  Reference    N
```

CHAPTER

5

Using the XML Engine to Transport SAS Data Sets across Operating Environments

What Is Transporting a SAS Data Set?

Transporting a SAS data set is the process of putting the file in a format in order to move it across hosts. The process consists of the following steps:

1 Export an XML document on the source host. The XML document contains the data and file attributes of one or more SAS data sets in XML markup. To export an XML document, use the LIBNAME statement and specify the XML engine, then use either the DATA step or COPY procedure.

2 Transfer the XML document to the target host. Transferring is the process of moving a file between hosts across a network. Various third-party products are available for performing this operation.

3 Translate the XML document to SAS proprietary format on the target host. To translate XML markup to SAS proprietary format, use the LIBNAME statement, specify the XML engine, then use either the DATA step or COPY procedure.

For more information about moving SAS files, see *Moving and Accessing SAS Files.*

Note: The XML engine supports features starting with SAS 7, such as long data set and variable names. For moving SAS data sets across operating environments, the XML engine does not replace the XPORT transport engine; however, the XPORT engine does not support these features. △

Transporting a SAS Data Set

This example exports an XML document from a SAS data set on a source host, then imports the XML document to a SAS data set on a target host. The XML engine uses all defaults; for example, the format is GENERIC, which is a simple, well-formed XML markup. The COPY procedure is used to read the SAS data set and write its content in XML markup, then the DATA step is used to read the XML document and write its content to a SAS data set.

The following output shows the SAS data set MYFILES.CLASS to be moved to another host.

Output 5.1   SAS Data Set MYFILES.CLASS to Be Exported

```
         Obs    Name      Sex    Age    Height    Weight

          1     Alfred     M      14     69.0     112.5
          2     Alice      F      13     56.5      84.0
          3     Barbara    F      13     65.3      98.0
          4     Carol      F      14     62.8     102.5
          5     Henry      M      14     63.5     102.5
          6     James      M      12     57.3      83.0
          7     Jane       F      12     59.8      84.5
          8     Janet      F      15     62.5     112.5
          9     Jeffrey    M      13     62.5      84.0
         10     John       M      12     59.0      99.5
         11     Joyce      F      11     51.3      50.5
         12     Judy       F      14     64.3      90.0
         13     Louise     F      12     56.3      77.0
         14     Mary       F      15     66.5     112.0
         15     Philip     M      16     72.0     150.0
         16     Robert     M      12     64.8     128.0
         17     Ronald     M      15     67.0     133.0
         18     Thomas     M      11     57.5      85.0
         19     William    M      15     66.5     112.0
```

The following SAS program exports an XML document on the source host for the SAS data set MYFILES.CLASS:

```
libname myfiles 'SAS-library'; ❶

libname trans xml 'XML-document'; ❷

proc copy in=myfiles out=trans; ❸
   select class;
run;
```

1 The first LIBNAME statement assigns the libref MYFILES to the physical location of the SAS library that stores the SAS data set CLASS in SAS proprietary format. The V9 engine is the default.

2 The second LIBNAME statement assigns the libref TRANS to the physical location of the file (complete pathname, filename, and file extension) that will store the exported XML document, and then specifies the XML engine. By default, the XML engine generates GENERIC format.

3 The COPY procedure reads the SAS data set MYFILES.CLASS and writes its content in XML markup to the specified file.

Here is the resulting XML document.

Output 5.2   XML Document Exported from MYFILES.CLASS

```
<?xml version="1.0" encoding="windows-1252" ?>
<TABLE>
   <CLASS>
      <Name> Alfred </Name>
      <Sex> M </Sex>
      <Age> 14 </Age>
      <Height> 69 </Height>
      <Weight> 112.5 </Weight>
   </CLASS>
   <CLASS>
      <Name> Alice </Name>
      <Sex> F </Sex>
      <Age> 13 </Age>
      <Height> 56.5 </Height>
      <Weight> 84 </Weight>
   </CLASS>
      .
      .
      .

   <CLASS>
      <Name> William </Name>
      <Sex> M </Sex>
      <Age> 15 </Age>
      <Height> 66.5 </Height>
      <Weight> 112 </Weight>
   </CLASS>
</TABLE>
```

After the XML document is exported on the source host, it must be transferred from the source host to the target host. Then, with the XML document available on the target host, the following SAS program translates the XML markup to SAS proprietary format:

```
libname trans xml 'XML-document'; ❶

libname myfiles 'SAS-library'; ❷

data myfiles.class; ❸
   set trans.class;
run;
```

1 The first LIBNAME statement assigns the libref TRANS to the physical location of the XML document (complete pathname, filename, and file extension) that was transferred to the target host, and specifies the XML engine. By default, the XML engine expects GENERIC format.

2 The second LIBNAME statement assigns the libref MYFILES to the physical location of the SAS library that will store the resulting SAS data set. The V9 engine is the default.

3 The DATA step reads the XML document and writes its content in SAS proprietary format.

Issuing the PRINT procedure produces the output for the data set that was translated from the XML document:

```
proc print data=myfiles.class;
run;
```

Output 5.3   PROC PRINT Output for MYFILES.CLASS Moved to Another Host by Importing XML Document

```
                        The SAS System                              1

        Obs     WEIGHT      HEIGHT        AGE     SEX     NAME

         1      112.5        69.0          14      M      Alfred
         2       84.0        56.5          13      F      Alice
         3       98.0        65.3          13      F      Barbara
         4      102.5        62.8          14      F      Carol
         5      102.5        63.5          14      M      Henry
         6       83.0        57.3          12      M      James
         7       84.5        59.8          12      F      Jane
         8      112.5        62.5          15      F      Janet
         9       84.0        62.5          13      M      Jeffrey
        10       99.5        59.0          12      M      John
        11       50.5        51.3          11      F      Joyce
        12       90.0        64.3          14      F      Judy
        13       77.0        56.3          12      F      Louise
        14      112.0        66.5          15      F      Mary
        15      150.0        72.0          16      M      Philip
        16      128.0        64.8          12      M      Robert
        17      133.0        67.0          15      M      Ronald
        18       85.0        57.5          11      M      Thomas
        19      112.0        66.5          15      M      William
```

Understanding and Using Tagsets for the XML Engine

What Is a Tagset?

A tagset specifies instructions for generating a markup language from your SAS data set. The resulting output contains embedded instructions in order to define layout and some content. SAS provides tagsets for a variety of markup languages, which includes XML.

SAS Tagsets

SAS provides tagset definitions for a variety of markup language output. SAS supplies several tagsets for XML output. That is, when you specify the format type with XMLTYPE=, the XML engine uses a specific tagset for the XML output. For example, XMLTYPE=GENERIC uses Tagsets.Sasxmog.

You can override the default tagset that is used for a format type by using the TAGSET= option and specifying a tagset. There are several SAS tagsets that are associated with the XML engine. Currently, the tagset names that begin with SAS are associated with the XML engine:

Tagsets.Sasxmacc2002
> supports the Microsoft Access 2002 database.

Tagsets.Sasxmacc2003
> supports the Microsoft Access 2003 database.

Tagsets.Sasxmiss
> produces an empty element start tag and end tag for a missing value.

Tagsets.Sasxmnmis
> does not generate element tags for a missing value. That is, if a variable contains a missing value, the XML engine does not generate an element occurrence.

Tagsets.Sasxmnsp
> does not pad PCDATA with blanks. For an example, see "Using a SAS Tagset to Remove White Spaces in Output XML Markup" on page 73.

Tagsets.Sasxmog

produces XML markup that is similar to the Oracle8iXML implementation used by Oracle but is more generic. This is the tagset used by the GENERIC format type.

Tagsets.Sasxmoh

produces very simple HTML markup. This is the tagset used by the HTML format type.

Tagsets.Sasxmor

produces XML markup that is equivalent to the Oracle8iXML implementation, which is used by Oracle. This is the tagset used by the ORACLE format type.

Tagsets.sasFMT

produces XML markup for FORMAT and INFORMAT metadata generation.

Tagsets.sasxmdtd

for export only, produces an embedded DTD (Document Type Definition) in the body of the data markup. Note that DTDs are obsolete and XML Schema will be the only fully supported form in future releases.

Tagsets.sasxmxsd

for exporting only, produces an embedded XSD (W3C XML Schema) in the body of the data markup.

To get a current list of tagsets, issue the following SAS statements:

```
proc template;
   list tagsets;
```

To view the definition for a tagset, issue the following SAS statements:

```
proc template;
   source tagset-name;
```

CAUTION:

Use the XML engine tagsets outside of the engine with caution. Even though you can specify the tagsets that are associated with the XML engine for ODS output, those tagsets were designed specifically for the XML engine. The results of specifying them for ODS MARKUP output might not be suitable. △

Creating Customized Tagsets

In addition to using the tagsets provided by SAS, you can modify the SAS tagsets, and you can create your own tagsets. To create a tagset, use the TEMPLATE procedure in order to define the tagset definition. For information about creating customized tagsets, see PROC TEMPLATE in the *SAS Output Delivery System User's Guide*.

For an example, see "Defining and Using a Customized Tagset to Use Labels in Node Names" on page 74.

CAUTION:

Use customized tagsets with caution. If you are unfamiliar with XML output, do not specify different tagsets. If you alter the tagset when exporting an XML document and then attempt to import the XML document generated by that altered tagset, the XML engine might not be able to translate the XML markup back to SAS proprietary format. △

Using a SAS Tagset to Remove White Spaces in Output XML Markup

This example uses a SAS tagset in order to generate customized XML output. The default tagset for XMLTYPE=GENERIC is Tagsets.Sasxmog, which adds an extra space (padding) to the beginning and end of each output XML element.

The customized tagset Tagsets.Sasxmnsp, which is supplied by SAS, does not include the white space. The example uses the data set SASHELP.CLASS.

These statements specify the SAS tagset Tagsets.Sasxmnsp and generate the following XML output. Only the first observation (row) is shown.

```
libname testxml xml 'C:\My Documents\XML\nospace.xml' tagset=tagsets.sasxmnsp;

proc copy in=sashelp out=testxml;
   select class;
run;
```

Output 6.1 XML Document NOSPACE.XML

```
 <?xml version="1.0" encoding="windows-1252" ?>
- <TABLE>
 -- <CLASS>
    <Name>Alfred</Name>
    <Sex>M</Sex>
    <Age>14</Age>
    <Height>69</Height>
    <Weight>112.5</Weight>
    </CLASS>
```

To compare the results, these statements use the default tagset, which is Tagsets.Sasxmog, and generate the following XML output GENERIC.XML:

```
libname xmlgenr xml 'C:\My Documents\XML\generic.xml';

proc copy in=sashelp out=xmlgenr;
   select class;
run;
```

Output 6.2 XML Document GENERIC.XML

```
 <?xml version="1.0" encoding="windows-1252" ?>
- <TABLE>
 -- <CLASS>
    <Name> Alfred </Name>
    <Sex> M </Sex>
    <Age> 14 </Age>
    <Height> 69 </Height>
    <Weight> 112.5 </Weight>
    </CLASS>
```

Defining and Using a Customized Tagset to Use Labels in Node Names

This example defines a customized tagset in order to generate XML output that uses labels rather than the variable names in node names. The default tagset for XMLTYPE=GENERIC is Tagsets.Sasxmog, which uses variable names. The customized tagset uses labels.

Note: When you use customized tagsets, especially when exporting an XML document, be sure that you produce valid XML markup. While this example uses labels as XML element tags, labels might not be appropriate, for example, if they contain quotation marks, embedded blanks, special characters, and so on. △

First, the following code creates the data set WORK.SINGERS:

```
data Singers;
   input Name $ Style $;
   label Name="SingerFirstName"
      Style="MusicStyle";
   datalines;
Tom Rock
Kris Country
Willie Country
Barbra Contemporary
Paul Rock
Randy Country
;
```

The following code defines the new tagset Tagsets.Uselabs:

```
proc template;
     define tagset Tagsets.Uselabs;
     parent = tagsets.sasxmog;
     notes "Uses label instead of name for tags";
     define event SASColumn;
       start:
       ndent;
       put     '<' ;
       put     TEXT           / if cmp(XMLDATAFORM, "ATTRIBUTE");
       put     ' name="'       / if cmp(XMLDATAFORM, "ATTRIBUTE");
       put     LABEL;
       put     '"'            / if cmp(XMLDATAFORM, "ATTRIBUTE");
       break;
       finish:
       xdent                  / if exists(MISSING);
       break                  / if exists(MISSING);
       put     ' />'           / if cmp(XMLDATAFORM, "ATTRIBUTE");
       put     CR             / if cmp(XMLDATAFORM, "ATTRIBUTE");
       xdent                  / if cmp(XMLDATAFORM, "ATTRIBUTE");
       break                  / if cmp(XMLDATAFORM, "ATTRIBUTE");
       put     '</' ;
       put     LABEL;
       put     '>' ;
       put     CR;
       xdent;
       break;
     end;
```

```
        end; /* uselabs */
    run;
```

These statements specify the customized tagset Tagsets.Uselabs and generate the following XML output Labels.XML:

```
libname testxml xml 'C:\My Documents\XML\labels.xml' tagset=tagsets.uselabs;

proc copy in=work out=testxml;
    select Singers;
run;
```

Output 6.3   XML Document Labels.XML

```
<?xml version="1.0" encoding="windows-1252" ?>
<TABLE>
   <SINGERS>
      <SingerFirstName> Tom </SingerFirstName>
      <MusicStyle> Rock </MusicStyle>
   </SINGERS>
   <SINGERS>
      <SingerFirstName> Kris </SingerFirstName>
      <MusicStyle> Country </MusicStyle>
   </SINGERS>
   <SINGERS>
      <SingerFirstName> Willie </SingerFirstName>
      <MusicStyle> Country </MusicStyle>
   </SINGERS>
   <SINGERS>
      <SingerFirstName> Barbra </SingerFirstName>
      <MusicStyle> Contempo </MusicStyle>
   </SINGERS>
   <SINGERS>
      <SingerFirstName> Paul </SingerFirstName>
      <MusicStyle> Rock </MusicStyle>
   </SINGERS>
   <SINGERS>
      <SingerFirstName> Randy </SingerFirstName>
      <MusicStyle> Country </MusicStyle>
   </SINGERS>
</TABLE>
```

To compare the results, these statements use the default tagset, which is Tagsets.Sasxmog, and generate the following XML output GENERIC.XML:

```
libname xmlgenr xml 'C:\My Documents\XML\generic.xml' xmltype=generic;

proc copy in=work out=xmlgenr;
    select Singers;
run;
```

Output 6.4   XML Document GENERIC.XML

```
<?xml version="1.0" encoding="windows-1252" ?>
<TABLE>
   <SINGERS>
      <Name> Tom </Name>
      <Style> Rock </Style>
   </SINGERS>
   <SINGERS>
      <Name> Kris </Name>
      <Style> Country </Style>
   </SINGERS>
   <SINGERS>
      <Name> Willie </Name>
      <Style> Country </Style>
   </SINGERS>
   <SINGERS>
      <Name> Barbra </Name>
      <Style> Contempo </Style>
   </SINGERS>
   <SINGERS>
      <Name> Paul </Name>
      <Style> Rock </Style>
   </SINGERS>
   <SINGERS>
      <Name> Randy </Name>
      <Style> Country </Style>
   </SINGERS>
</TABLE>
```

Defining and Using a Customized Tagset to Export an HTML Document

This example defines a customized tagset in order to generate HTML output.
First, the following code creates the data set WORK.SINGERS:

```
data Singers;
   input Name $ Style $;
   label Name="SingerFirstName"
      Style="MusicStyle";
   datalines;
Tom Rock
Kris Country
Willie Country
Barbra Contemporary
Paul Rock
Randy Country
;
```

The following code defines the new tagset Tagsets.Enghtml:

```
proc template;
   define tagset tagsets.engHTML;
      parent = tagsets.sasxmog;
      notes "SAS XML LIBNAME Engine simple HTML table";

      define event doc;
      start:
         put '<!DOCTYPE HTML PUBLIC "-//W3C//DTD HTML 3.2 Final//EN">' CR;
```

```
      put '<HTML>' CR;
      break;
  finish:
      put '</HTML>' CR;
      break;
  end;

  define event doc_body;
  start:
      ndent;
      put '<BODY>' CR;
      break;
  finish:
      put '</BODY>' CR;
      xdent;
      break;
  end;

  define event table;
  start:
      ndent;
      put  '<TABLE border="1" width="100%">' CR;
      break;
  finish:
      put  '</TABLE>' CR;
      xdent;
      break;
  end;

  define event colspecs;
  start:
      break / if cmp(XMLMETADATA, "NONE");
      ndent;
      put '<THEAD>' CR;
      ndent;
      put '<TR>' CR;
      ndent;
      break;
  finish:
      break / if cmp(XMLMETADATA, "NONE");
      xdent;
      put '</TR>' CR;
      xdent;
      put '</THEAD>' CR;
      xdent;
      break;
  end;

  define event colspec_entry;
```

```
                  break / if cmp(XMLMETADATA, "NONE");
                  put '<TH> ';
                  put NAME;
                  put ' </TH>' CR;
                  break;
               end;

            define event table_body;
            start:
               ndent;
               put "<TBODY>" CR;
               break;
             finish:
               put "</TBODY>" CR;
               xdent;
               break;
            end;

            define event SASRow;
            start:
               ndent;
               put '<TR>' CR;
               break;
            finish:
               put '</TR>' CR;
               xdent;
               break;
            end;

            define event SASColumn;
            start:
               ndent;
               put '<TD' ;
               break;
            finish:
               put '</TD>' CR ;
               xdent;
               break;
            end;

            define event MLEVDAT;
               put '>' ;
               put ' ';
               put VALUE;
               put ' ';
               break;
            end;
        end; /* engHTML */
     run;
```

These statements specify the customized tagset Tagsets.Enghtml and generate the HTML output that follows:

```
libname myhtml xml 'C:\My Documents\HTML\testhtml.html' tagset=tagsets.enghtml;

proc copy in=work out=myhtml;
    select Singers;
run;
```

Output 6.5 HTML Output for Testhtml.HTML

```
<!DOCTYPE HTML PUBLIC "-//W3C//DTD HTML 3.2 Final//EN">
<HTML>
    <BODY>
        <TABLE border="1" width="100%">
            <TBODY>
                <TR>
                    <TD> Tom </TD>
                    <TD> Rock </TD>
                </TR>
                <TR>
                    <TD> Kris </TD>
                    <TD> Country </TD>
                </TR>
                <TR>
                    <TD> Willie </TD>
                    <TD> Country </TD>
                </TR>
                <TR>
                    <TD> Barbra </TD>
                    <TD> Contempo </TD>
                </TR>
                <TR>
                    <TD> Paul </TD>
                    <TD> Rock </TD>
                </TR>
                <TR>
                    <TD> Randy </TD>
                    <TD> Country </TD>
                </TR>
            </TBODY>
</TABLE>
</BODY>
</HTML>
```

P A R T *2*

Reference

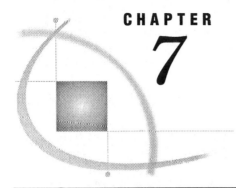

LIBNAME Statement for the XML Engine

Using the LIBNAME Statement

For the XML engine, the LIBNAME statement associates a SAS libref with an XML document in order to import or export the XML document.

For basic examples, see Chapter 3, "Importing XML Documents," on page 29 and Chapter 2, "Exporting XML Documents," on page 9.

LIBNAME Statement Syntax

LIBNAME *libref* **XML** <*'XML-document-path'* > <*XML-engine-options*>;

Arguments

libref
   is a valid SAS name that serves as a shortcut name to associate with the physical location of the XML document. The name must conform to the rules for SAS names. A libref cannot exceed eight characters.

   Limitation: The maximum number of concurrent open librefs that you can have assigned to the XML engine is 20.

XML
   is the engine name for the SAS XML engine that imports and exports an XML document.

   Note: At your site, the XML engine name could be different if your system administrator assigned a different nickname to the XML engine. See your system administrator for the correct XML engine nickname. △

'*XML-document-path*'
   is the physical location of the XML document for export or import. Include the
   complete pathname, the filename, and the file extension. An example is
   `'C:\My Documents\XML\myfile.xml'`. Enclose the physical name in single or
   double quotation marks.

   Requirement: The external file specification must be a file, not a folder. The .xml
   extension is not assumed.

   Tip: You can use the FILENAME statement in order to assign a fileref to be
   associated with the physical location of the XML document to be exported or
   imported.
   If the fileref matches the libref, then you do not need to specify the physical
   location of the XML document in the LIBNAME statement. For example, the
   following code writes to the XML document Fred.XML:

```
filename bedrock 'C:\XMLdata\fred.xml';

libname bedrock xml;

proc print data=bedrock.fred;
run;
```

   To specify a fileref for the XML document that does not match the libref, you
   can use the XMLFILEREF=*fileref* option. For example, the following code writes
   to the XML document Wilma.XML:

```
filename cartoon 'C:\XMLdata\wilma.xml';

libname bedrock xml xmlfileref=cartoon;

proc print data=bedrock.wilma;
run;
```

XML Engine Options

The following options are the basic options for the XML engine:

INDENT=*integer*
   specifies the number of columns to indent each nested element in the exported
   XML document. The value can be from 0 (which specifies no indentation) through
   32. This is a cosmetic specification, which is ignored by an XML-enabled browser.

   Default: 3

   Restriction: Use this option when exporting an XML document only.

FORMATACTIVE=YES | NO
   specifies whether CDISC ODM CodeList elements, which contain instructions for
   transcoding display data in a CDISC ODM document, are to be converted to SAS
   variable formats, and vice versa.
   In an import operation, specifying FORMATACTIVE=YES converts the CDISC
   ODM CodeList elements to the corresponding SAS formats, registers the SAS
   formats on the referenced variables, and stores the created SAS formats in the
   format catalog.
   In an export operation, specifying FORMATACTIVE=YES converts SAS formats
   to the corresponding CDISC ODM CodeList elements.
   In both import and export operations, specifying FORMATACTIVE=NO causes
   display data to be ignored.

Default: NO

Tip: By default, the format catalog is created in the Work library. If you want to store the catalog in a permanent library, use the FORMATLIBRARY= option.

Tip: When the format catalog is updated, the default behavior is for new SAS formats that are created by translating CDISC ODM CodeList elements to replace any existing SAS formats that have the same name. To prevent existing formats from being overwritten, specify FORMATNOREPLACE=YES.

FORMATLIBRARY=*libref*
specifies the libref of an existing SAS library in which to create the format catalog.

Restriction: Use this option only if you are importing from the CDISC ODM format type (that is, when you have specified XMLTYPE=CDISCODM) and when you have specified FORMATACTIVE=YES.

FORMATNOREPLACE=YES | NO
specifies whether to replace existing format entries in the format catalog search path in cases where an existing format entry has the same name as a format that is being created by the XML engine when it converts a CDISC ODM CodeList element.

When FORMATNOREPLACE=YES, the engine does not replace formats that have the same name.

When FORMATNOREPLACE=NO, the engine replaces formats that have the same name.

Restriction: Use this option only when you are importing an XML document that is in CDISC ODM format (that is, when you have specified XMLTYPE=CDISCODM).

Default: NO

OIMSTART=*nnn*
specifies a beginning reference number, which in the exported XML document will be incremented sequentially for catalog, schema, table, and column identification.

Default: 1

Deprecated: The OIMSTART= option is deprecated in SAS 9. The option will not be supported in a future release. Functionality will be provided with a different option.

XMLCONCATENATE | XMLCONCAT=NO | YES
specifies whether the file to be imported contains multiple, concatenated XML documents. Importing concatenated XML documents is useful, for example, if an application is producing a complete document per query/response as in a Web form.

Default: NO

Restriction: Use this option when importing an XML document only.

Restriction: Use XMLCONCATENATE=YES cautiously. If an XML document consists of concatenated XML documents, the content is not standard XML construction. The option is provided for convenience, not to encourage invalid XML format.

Featured in: "Importing Concatenated XML Documents" on page 37.

XMLDATAFORM=ELEMENT | ATTRIBUTE
specifies whether the tag for the element to contain SAS variable information (name and data) is in open element or enclosed attribute format. For example, if the variable name is PRICE and the value of one observation is `1.98`, the generated output for ELEMENT is `<PRICE> 1.98 </PRICE>` and for ATTRIBUTE it is `<COLUMN name="PRICE" value="1.98" />`.

Default: ELEMENT

Restriction: Use this option when exporting an XML document only.

XMLDOUBLE=FORMAT | PRECISION

determines the precision of a numeric value by specifying whether you want the value to be controlled by an assigned SAS format or whether you want the stored raw value.

In SAS, numeric variables store values in floating-point format. Rarely though do you display numeric values as they are stored. Usually, a numeric variable has an assigned SAS format, which controls the written appearance of the values, making them more readable. For example, if the stored value is 12345.1234 and the SAS format best8.2 is assigned to the variable, SAS displays the value as 12345.12. When written, the SAS format reduces the number of digits.

When a numeric variable has an assigned SAS format, the default behavior of the XML engine is that the format controls the numeric values that are imported or exported. For example, using the stored value and SAS format example above, if you exported the value to an XML document, by default, the XML element would contain the truncated value 12345.12, not the stored raw value.

FORMAT

uses an assigned SAS format in order to control the value:

When exporting, the XML engine uses the assigned SAS format in order to control the values for a numeric variable. Note that an assigned SAS format could reduce the number of digits for a numeric value in the output.

When importing, the XML engine retrieves PCDATA (parsable character data) from the named element.

PRECISION

retains the precision of numeric values:

When exporting, the XML engine generates an attribute-value pair (of the form `rawvalue="value"`). SAS uses the base64 encoding of the stored machine representation. (The base64 encoding method converts binary data into ASCII text and vice versa and is similar to the MIME format.)

When importing, the XML engine retrieves the value from the rawvalue= attribute in the element, ignoring the PCDATA content of the element. Typically, you would use XMLDOUBLE=PRECISION to import an XML document when data content is more important than readability.

Default: FORMAT

Featured in: "Exporting Numeric Values" on page 18 and "Importing an XML Document with Numeric Values" on page 31.

XMLFILEREF=*fileref*

is the SAS name that is associated with the physical location of the XML document to be exported or imported. To assign the fileref, use the FILENAME statement. For example, the following code writes to the XML document Wilma.XML:

```
filename cartoon 'C:\XMLdata\wilma.xml';

libname bedrock xml xmlfileref=cartoon;

proc print data=bedrock.wilma;
run;
```

Tip: The XML engine can access any data referenced by a fileref assigned by the FILENAME statement, including the URL access method.

XMLMETA=DATA | SCHEMADATA | SCHEMA
specifies whether to include metadata-related information in the exported markup, or specifies whether to import metadata-related information that is included in the input XML document.

Metadata-related information is metadata that describes the characteristics (types, lengths, levels, and so on) of columns within the table markup. Including the metadata-related information can be useful when exporting an XML document from a SAS data set to process on an external product.

DATA
ignores metadata-related information. DATA includes only data content in the exported markup and imports only data content in the input XML document.

SCHEMADATA
includes both data content and metadata-related information in the exported markup and imports both data content and metadata-related information in the input XML document.

SCHEMA
ignores data content. SCHEMA includes only metadata-related information in the exported markup and imports only metadata-related information in the input XML document.

Default: DATA

Aliases:

DATA   NONE, NO, IGNORE

SCHEMADATA   FULL, YES

Restriction: Use this option for the HTML and MSACCESS formats only.

Interaction: For XMLMETA=SCHEMADATA, if XMLSCHEMA= is specified, separate metadata-related information is written to the physical location specified with XMLSCHEMA=. The data content is written to the physical location of the XML document specified in the LIBNAME statement. If XMLSCHEMA= is not specified, the metadata-related information is embedded with the data content in the XML document.

Featured in: "Exporting an XML Document Containing a SAS User-Defined Format" on page 11 and "Exporting an XML Document Containing SAS Dates, Times, and Datetimes" on page 15.

Note: Prior to SAS 9, the functionality for the XMLMETA= option used the keyword XMLSCHEMA=. SAS 9 changed XMLSCHEMA= to XMLMETA=. SAS 9.1 continues the functionality for XMLMETA= and adds new functionality using XMLSCHEMA=. △

XMLPROCESS=CONFORM | RELAX
determines how the XML engine processes character data that does not conform to W3C specifications.

CONFORM
requires that the XML conform to W3C specifications. W3C specifications state that for character data, certain characters such as the left angle bracket (<), the ampersand (&), and the apostrophe (') must be escaped using character references or strings like **&**. For example, to allow attribute values to contain both single and double quotation marks, the apostrophe or single-quotation mark character (') can be represented as **'** and the double-quotation mark character (") can be represented as **"**.

RELAX

allows for character data that does not conform to W3C specifications to be accepted. That is, non-escaped characters such as the apostrophe, double quotation marks, and the ampersand are accepted in character data.

Restriction: Non-escaped angle brackets in character data are not accepted.

Restriction: Use XMLPROCESS=RELAX cautiously. If an XML document consists of non-escaped characters, the content is not standard XML construction. The option is provided for convenience, not to encourage invalid XML format.

Default: CONFORM

Featured in: "Importing an XML Document with Non-Escaped Character Data" on page 32.

XMLSCHEMA=*fileref*|*'external-file'*

specifies an external file to contain metadata-related information.

fileref

is the SAS name that is associated with the physical location of the output file. To assign a fileref, use the FILENAME statement.

'external-file'

is the physical location of the file to contain the metadata-related information. Include the complete pathname and the filename. Enclose the physical name in single or double quotation marks.

Restriction: Use this option when exporting an XML document only and with XMLMETA=SCHEMADATA specified.

Restriction: Use this option for the GENERIC and MSACCESS formats only.

Interaction: If XMLMETA=SCHEMADATA and XMLSCHEMA= is specified, the data is written to the physical location of the XML document specified in the LIBNAME statement, and separate metadata-related information is written to the physical location specified with XMLSCHEMA=. If XMLSCHEMA= is not specified, the metadata-related information is embedded with the data content in the XML document.

Featured in: "Exporting an XML Document with Separate Metadata" on page 23.

XMLTYPE=GENERIC | ORACLE | OIMDBM | EXPORT | HTML | MSACCESS | CDISCODM

specifies the format type:

Default: GENERIC

Tip: You can control the markup by specifying options such as INDENT=, XMLDATAFORM=, XMLMETA= (when applicable), and TAGSET=.

GENERIC

a simple, well-formed XML format. The XML document consists of a root (enclosing) element and repeating element instances as shown in the following XML document. GENERIC determines a variable's attributes from the data.

Requirement: When importing, the GENERIC format type requires a specific physical structure. See "Understanding the Required Physical Structure for an XML Document to Be Imported Using the GENERIC Format Type" on page 45.

Featured in: "Exporting an XML Document Containing SAS Dates, Times, and Datetimes" on page 15, "Exporting Numeric Values" on page 18, "Importing an XML Document Using the GENERIC Format Type" on page 29, and several examples throughout the document.

ORACLE

is the XML format for the markup standards equivalent to the Oracle8iXML implementation, as shown in the following XML document. The number of columns to indent each nested element is one, and the enclosing element tag for the contents of the SAS data set is ROWSET.

Featured in: "Exporting an XML Document for Use by Oracle" on page 9.

OIMDBM

is the XML format for the markup standards supported by the Open Information Model (Database Schema Model) proposed by the Metadata Coalition (MDC) as vendor and technology independent, conforming to the 1.0 specification. The XML markup contains metadata that is used in operational and data warehousing environments.

Deprecated: The OIMDBM format type is deprecated in SAS 9. The format type will not be supported in a future release. Functionality will be provided with a different format type.

EXPORT

is an alias to specify the XML format that is most commonly used in the industry. In SAS 9.1, specifying XMLTYPE=EXPORT is the same as specifying XMLTYPE=OIMDBM. Future releases will upgrade this format specification as needed.

HTML

is the HyperText Markup Language format. The XML engine generates HTML table markup, intended to facilitate viewing data in a tabular format.

Restriction: XMLTYPE=HTML is available for exporting only.

Deprecated: The HTML type is deprecated beginning in SAS 9.1.3. The HTML type will not be supported in some future release. Equivalent functionality can be achieved by specifying a tagset. See "Defining and Using a Customized Tagset to Export an HTML Document" on page 76.

MSACCESS

is the XML format for the markup standards supported for a Microsoft Access database (.mdb). If the Microsoft Access file contains metadata-related information, then you must specify MSACCESS rather than the default GENERIC format type. If there is an embedded XML schema, specifying MSACCESS and the XMLMETA=SCHEMADATA option causes a variable's attributes to be obtained from the embedded schema. If there is not an embedded schema, MSACCESS uses default values for attributes.

Interaction: When importing, MSACCESS supports Microsoft Access 2002 and 2003 databases. When exporting, use the TAGSET= option and specify TAGSETS.SASXMAC2002 for Microsoft Access 2002 or TAGSETS.SASXMAC2003 for Microsoft Access 2003.

Featured in: "Importing an XML Document Created by Microsoft Access" on page 34.

CDISCODM

is the XML format for the markup standards that are defined in the Operational Data Model (ODM) that was created by the Clinical Data Interchange Standards Consortium (CDISC). The XML engine supports the ODM 1.2 schema specification. ODM supports the electronic acquisition, exchange, and archiving of clinical trials data and metadata for medical and biopharmaceutical product development.

Tip: Use the FORMATACTIVE=, FORMATNOREPLACE=, and FORMATLIBRARY= options to specify how display data are read and stored in the target environment.

Featured in: "Importing a CDISC ODM Document" on page 39 and "Exporting an XML Document in CDISC ODM Format" on page 27.

Statement Options for National Language Support

The following options are for National Language Support (NLS), which is the ability of a software program to handle more than one language, country, and cultural setting.

CAUTION:

These options should be used with caution. If you are unfamiliar with character sets, encoding methods, or translation tables, do not use these options without proper technical advice. △

ODSCHARSET=*character-set*

specifies the character set to use for the output file. A character set includes letters, logograms, digits, punctuation, symbols, and control characters that are used for display and printing. An example of a character set is ISO-8859-1.

Restriction: Use this option when exporting an XML document only.

Tip: The combination of the character set and translation table (encoding method) results in the file's encoding.

See: For more information about character sets, see the *SAS National Language Support (NLS): User's Guide*.

ODSTRANTAB=*table-name*

specifies the translation table to use for the output file. The translation table (encoding method) is a set of rules that are used to map characters in a character set to numeric values. An example of a translation table is one that converts characters from EBCDIC to ASCII-ISO. The *table-name* can be any translation table that SAS provides or any user-defined translation table. The value must be the name of a SAS catalog entry in either the SASUSER.PROFILE catalog or the SASHELP.HOST catalog.

Restriction: Use this option when exporting an XML document only.

Tip: The combination of the character set and translation table results in the file's encoding.

See: For more information on translation tables, see the *SAS National Language Support (NLS): User's Guide*.

XMLENCODING=*encoding-value*

overrides the SAS data set's encoding for the output file.

Restriction: Use this option when exporting an XML document only.

Tip: The combination of the character set and translation table (encoding method) results in the file's encoding.

Tip: When using FTP to transfer an exported XML document, transfer the file in ASCII (text) mode if you used the default encoding or binary mode if you specified an encoding value.

See: For more information about encoding and a list of encoding values, see the *SAS National Language Support (NLS): User's Guide*.

XML Engine Advanced Options

The following advanced options provide customization:

METAPASS=*password*
specifies the password that corresponds to the user identification on the SAS Metadata Server. The maximum length is 512 characters.
The network protocol determines whether a password is required. If the protocol is COM, a password is not required; if the protocol is BRIDGE (which is the default), a password is required. If this option is not specified and the protocol is BRIDGE, the value is obtained from the METAPASS= system option. See the *SAS Language Reference: Dictionary* for information on the METAPASS= system option.

METAPORT=*number*
specifies the TCP port that the SAS Metadata Server is listening to for connections. An example is **metaport=5282**.
The network protocol determines whether a port number is required. If the protocol is COM, a port number is not required. If the protocol is BRIDGE (which is the default), a port number is required. If this option is not specified and the protocol is BRIDGE, the value is obtained from the METAPORT= system option or defaults to **9999**. See *SAS Language Reference: Dictionary* for information on the METAPORT= system option.

METAREPOSITORY=*name*
specifies the name that is assigned to a specific SAS Metadata Repository to use on the SAS Metadata Server. The maximum length is 32,000 characters. An example is **metarepository=myrepos**. If a name is not specified, the value is obtained from the METAREPOSITORY= system option. See the *SAS Language Reference: Dictionary* for information on the METAREPOSITORY= system option.

METASERVER=*address*
specifies the network IP (Internet Protocol) address of the computer that hosts the SAS Metadata Server. An example is **metaserver=d441.na.sas.com**. The maximum length is 256 characters.
The network protocol determines whether an IP address is required. If the protocol is COM and the server is on a local machine, an IP address is not required. If the protocol is COM and the server is not local (DCOM services) or the protocol is BRIDGE, an IP address is required. If this option is not specified and the protocol is specified as COM on the LIBNAME statement, this indicates a local server and no IP address will be used to connect to the server. Otherwise, if this option is not specified, the value is obtained from the METASERVER= system option. See the *SAS Language Reference: Dictionary* for information on the METASERVER= system option.

METAUSER=*id*
specifies the user identification for logging into the SAS Metadata Server. The maximum length is 256 characters.
The network protocol determines whether a user identification is required. If the protocol is COM, a user identification is not required; if the protocol is BRIDGE (which is the default), a user identification is required. If this option is not specified and the protocol is BRIDGE, the value is obtained from the METAUSER= system option. See the *SAS Language Reference: Dictionary* for information on the METAUSER= system option.

METAXMLMAP=*object-name*
is the name of a specific metadata object that is assigned to an XMLMap in a SAS Metadata Repository. The object defines the XMLMap, which is an XML document that you create that contains specific XMLMap syntax. The syntax tells the XML engine how to interpret the XML markup for importing or how to generate XML markup for exporting an XML document. The ID can be up to 17 characters. An example is `metaxmlmap="MyXMLMap"`. See "Using XMLMap Manager to Manage XMLMaps as Metadata Objects" on page 109 for information on how to import and create XMLMap metadata objects.

ODSRECSEP= DEFAULT | NONE | YES
controls the generation of a record separator that marks the end of a line in the output XML document.

DEFAULT
enables the XML engine to determine whether to generate a record separator based on the operating environment where you run the SAS job.
The use of a record separator varies by operating environment.

Recommendation: If you do not transport XML documents across environments, use the default behavior.

NONE
specifies to not generate a record separator.
The XML engine uses the logical record length of the file that you are writing to and writes one line of XML markup at a time to the output file.

Requirement: The logical record length of the file that you are writing to must be at least as long as the longest line that is produced. If the logical record length of the file is not long enough, then the markup might wrap to another line at an inappropriate place.

Limitation: Transporting an XML document that does not contain a record separator can be a problem. For example, FTP needs a record separator in order to transfer data properly in ASCII (text) mode.

YES
specifies to generate a record separator.

Tip: Most transfer utilities will interpret the record separator as a carriage return sequence. For example, using FTP in ASCII (text) mode to transport an XML document that contains a record separator results in properly constructed line breaks for the target environment.

Default: The XML engine determines whether to generate a record separator based on the operating environment where you run the SAS job.

Restriction: Use this option when exporting an XML document only.

TAGSET=*tagset-name*
specifies the name of a tagset in order to override the default tagset that is used by the format type specified with XMLTYPE=. For example, by default, XMLTYPE=GENERIC uses the tagset TAGSETS.SASXMOG, which uses the variable name to enclose the contents of a SAS variable (for example, **<STUDENT>** and **</STUDENT>**) and the name of the data set to enclose the contents of a SAS observation (for example, **<GRADES>** and **</GRADES>**). For more information on tagsets, see Chapter 6, "Understanding and Using Tagsets for the XML Engine," on page 71.
To change the tags that are produced, you can create a customized tagset and specify it with the TAGSET= option. For information about creating customized tagsets, see PROC TEMPLATE in the *The Complete Guide to the SAS Output Delivery System*.

Restriction: Use this option when exporting an XML document only.

Restriction: Use this option with caution. If you are unfamiliar with XML output formats, do not use this option.

Featured in: "Using a SAS Tagset to Remove White Spaces in Output XML Markup" on page 73 and "Defining and Using a Customized Tagset to Use Labels in Node Names" on page 74.

CAUTION:

If you alter the tagset when exporting an XML document and then attempt to import the XML document generated by that altered tagset, the XML engine might not be able to translate the XML markup back to SAS proprietary format. △

XMLMAP=*fileref* | *'XMLMap'*

specifies an XML document that you create that contains specific XMLMap syntax. The syntax tells the XML engine how to interpret the XML markup for importing. The XMLMap syntax is itself XML markup. See Chapter 8, "Creating an XMLMap," on page 95 for the XML tag names and descriptions.

fileref

is the SAS name that is associated with the physical location of the XMLMap. To assign a fileref, use the FILENAME statement.

'XMLMap'

is the physical location of the XMLMap. Include the complete pathname and the filename. It is suggested that you use the filename extension .map. Enclose the physical name in single or double quotation marks.

For example, the following statements import an XML document named MY.XML and specify the XMLMap named MY.MAP, which contains specific XMLMap syntax. The XML engine interprets the XML document as a SAS data set (table) named MY. In this example, XMLMAP= is used as an option in the LIBNAME statement:

```
libname test xml 'C:\XMLdata\my.xml' xmlmap='C:\XMLdata\my.map';

proc print data=test.my;
run;
```

Tip: You can also specify XMLMAP= as a data set option. The following example uses XMLMAP= as a data set option and also uses a fileref that is assigned to the XMLMap:

```
filename map 'C:\XMLdata\my.map';

libname test xml 'C:\XMLdata\my.xml';

proc print data=test.my (xmlmap=map);
run;
```

Featured in: Chapter 4, "Importing XML Documents Using an XMLMap," on page 45.

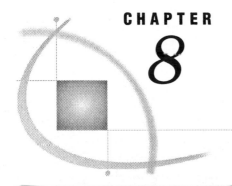

CHAPTER

8

Creating an XMLMap

Using XMLMap Syntax

The following topic contains the XML elements for the XMLMap syntax for Version 1.2. They are listed in the order in which you would typically code them in an XMLMap.

CAUTION:
The XMLMap markup, as XML itself, is case sensitive. The tag names must be uppercase, and the attributes must be lowercase. An example is **<SXLEMAP version="1.2">**. In addition, the supported XPath syntax is case sensitive as well. △

XMLMap Syntax Version 1.2

Element Descriptions

SXLEMAP version="*number*" name="*XMLMap*" description="*description*"
　　is the primary (root) enclosing element to contain the definition of the data set(s). The element provides the XML well-formed constraint for the definition(s).

Requirement:　The SXLEMAP element is required.

SXLEMAP has these attributes:

version="*number*"
: specifies the version of the XMLMap syntax. The documented syntax version is 1.2 and must be specified in order to obtain full functionality.

Default: The version= attribute default value is 1.0 and is retained for compatibility with prior releases of the XMLMap syntax. It is recommended that you update existing XMLMaps to Version 1.2.

Tip: To automatically update an XMLMap to Version 1.2, load the Version 1.0 or 1.1 XMLMap syntax into SAS XML Mapper, then save the file. For information on SAS XML Mapper, see "Using SAS XML Mapper to Generate and Update an XMLMap" on page 107.

name="*XMLMap*"
: is an optional attribute that specifies the filename of the XMLMap.

Tip: If you use the XMLMap Manager to import an XMLMap as a metadata object, the name= attribute value is used as the name for the metadata object. The name cannot be SXLEMAP or XMLMAP and must be unique to the repository. See "Using XMLMap Manager to Manage XMLMaps as Metadata Objects" on page 109.

description="*description*"
: is an optional attribute that specifies a description of the XMLMap.

The SXLEMAP element can contain one or more TABLE elements. For example,

```
<?xml version="1.0" ?>
<SXLEMAP version="1.2" name="Myxmlmap" description="sample XMLMap">
    <TABLE name="test1">
       .
       .
       .
    </TABLE>
    <TABLE name="test2">
       .
       .
       .
    </TABLE>
</SXLEMAP>
```

TABLE name="*data-set-name*"
: is an element to contain a data set definition. For example,

```
<TABLE name="channel">
```

Requirement: The TABLE element is required.

TABLE has this attribute:

name="*data-set-name*"
: specifies the name for the SAS data set. The name must be unique in the XMLMap definition, and the name must be a valid SAS name, which can be up to 32 characters.

Requirement: The name= attribute is required.

The TABLE element can contain one or more of the following elements that describe the data set attributes: TABLE-PATH, TABLE-END-PATH, TABLE-DESCRIPTION, and COLUMN.

TABLE-PATH syntax="*type*"

specifies a location path that tells the XML engine where in the XML document to locate and access specific elements in order to collect variables for the SAS data set. The location path defines the repeating element instances in the XML document, which is the SAS data set observation boundary. The observation boundary is translated into a collection of rows with a constant set of columns.

Requirement: The TABLE-PATH element is required.

TABLE-PATH has this attribute:

syntax="*type*"

is an optional attribute that specifies the type of syntax used in order to specify the location path. For all versions prior to and including Version 1.2, the supported syntax is a valid XPath construction in compliance with the World Wide Web Consortium (W3C) XPath specification.

Default: The default is XPath, that is, `syntax="xpath"`.

Requirement: The XPath construction is a formal specification that puts a path description similar to UNIX on each element of the XML structure. *Note that XPath syntax is case sensitive. For example, if an element tag name is uppercase, it must be uppercase in the location path; if it is lowercase, it must be lowercase.* All paths must begin with the root-enclosing element (denoted by a slash '/') or with the "any parent" variant (denoted by double slashes '//'). Other W3C documented forms are not currently supported.

For example, using the XML document RSS.XML, which is used in the example "Using an XMLMap to Import an XML Document as Multiple SAS Data Sets" on page 51, this TABLE-PATH element causes the following to occur:

```
<TABLE-PATH syntax="xpath"> /rss/channel/item </TABLE-PATH>
```

1 The XML engine reads the XML markup until it encounters the <ITEM> start tag.

2 The XML engine clears the input buffer, sets the contents to MISSING (by default), and scans elements for variable names based on the COLUMN element definitions. As values are encountered, they are read into the input buffer. (Note that whether the XML engine resets to MISSING is determined by the DEFAULT element as well as the COLUMN element retain= attribute.)

3 When the </ITEM> end tag is encountered, the XML engine writes the completed input buffer to the SAS data set as a SAS observation.

4 The process is repeated for each <ITEM> start-tag and </ITEM> end-tag sequence until the end-of-file is encountered in the input stream or until the TABLE-END-PATH (if specified) is achieved, which results in six observations.

CAUTION:
Specifying the table location path, which is the observation boundary, can be tricky due to start-tag and end-tag pairing. The table location path determines which end tag causes the XML engine to write the completed input buffer to the SAS data set. If you do not identify the appropriate end tag, the result could be concatenated data instead of separate observations, or an unexpected set of

columns. For examples, see "Determining the Observation Boundary to Avoid Concatenated Data" on page 61 and "Determining the Observation Boundary to Select the Best Columns" on page 64. △

TABLE-END-PATH syntax="*type*" beginend="Begin | End"
is an optional, optimization element that saves resources by stopping the processing of the XML document before the end of file. The location path tells the XML engine where in the XML document to locate and access a specific element in order to stop processing the XML document.

Default: Processing continues until the last end tag in the XML document.

Interaction: The TABLE-END-PATH element does not affect the observation boundary; that is determined with the TABLE-PATH element.

Tip: Specifying a location in order to stop processing is useful for XML documents that are hierarchical, but generally not appropriate for repeating instance data.

Featured in: "Using an XMLMap to Import an XML Document as Multiple SAS Data Sets" on page 51.

TABLE-END-PATH has these attributes:

syntax="*type*"
is an optional attribute that specifies the type of syntax used to specify the location path. For Version 1.2, the syntax is a valid XPath construction in compliance with the World Wide Web Consortium (W3C). The XPath form supported by the XML engine allows elements and attributes to be individually selected for exclusion in the generated SAS data set.

Default: The default is XPath, that is, `syntax="xpath"`.

Requirement: The XPath construction is a formal specification that puts a path description similar to UNIX on each element of the XML structure. *Note that XPath syntax is case sensitive. For example, if an element tag name is uppercase, it must be uppercase in the location path; if it is lowercase, it must be lowercase.* All paths must begin with the root-enclosing element (denoted by a slash '/') or with the "any parent" variant (denoted by double slashes '//'). Other W3C documented forms are not currently supported.

Featured in: "Using an XMLMap to Import an XML Document as Multiple SAS Data Sets" on page 51.

beginend="Begin | End"
is an optional attribute that specifies to stop processing when either the element start tag is encountered or the element end tag is encountered.

Default: The default is Begin.

For example, using the XML document RSS.XML, which is used in the example "Using an XMLMap to Import an XML Document as Multiple SAS Data Sets" on page 51, there is only one <CHANNEL> start-tag and one </CHANNEL> end-tag. With the TABLE-PATH location path,

```
<TABLE-PATH syntax="xpath"> /rss/channel </TABLE-PATH>
```

the XML engine would process the entire XML document, even though it does not store new data in the input buffer after it encounters the first <ITEM> start tag, because the remaining elements no longer qualify. The following TABLE-END-PATH location path tells the XML engine to stop processing when the <ITEM> start tag is encountered:

```
<TABLE-END-PATH syntax="xpath" beginend="Begin">
    /rss/channel/item </TABLE-END-PATH>
```

Therefore, with the two location path specifications, the XML engine processes only the highlighted data in the RSS.XML document for the CHANNEL data set, rather than the entire XML document:

```
<?xml version="1.0" encoding="ISO-8859-1" ?>
<rss version="0.91">
    <channel>
        <title>WriteTheWeb</title>
        <link>http://writetheweb.com</link>
        <description>News for web users that write back
            </description>
        <language>en-us</language>
        <copyright>Copyright 2000, WriteTheWeb team.
            </copyright>
        <managingEditor>editor@writetheweb.com
            </managingEditor>
        <webMaster>webmaster@writetheweb.com</webMaster>
        <image>
            <title>WriteTheWeb</title>
            <url>http://writetheweb.com/images/mynetscape88.gif
                </url>
            <link>http://writetheweb.com</link>
            <width>88</width>
            <height>31</height>
            <description>News for web users that write back
                </description>
        </image>
        <item>
            <title>Giving the world a pluggable Gnutella</title>
    <link>http://writetheweb.com/read.php?item=24</link>
            <description>WorldOS is a framework on which to build programs
                that work like Freenet or Gnutella-allowing distributed
                applications using  peer-to-peer routing.</description>
        </item>
        <item>
            .
            .
            .
    </channel>
</rss>
```

TABLE-DESCRIPTION

is an optional element that specifies a description for the data set, which can be up to 256 characters. This description is similar to the attribute that describes a data set, which you can assign with the DATASETS procedure using the LABEL= option in the MODIFY statement. For example,

```
<TABLE-DESCRIPTION> Data Set contains TV channel
    information </TABLE-DESCRIPTION>
```

COLUMN name="*name*" retain="NO|YES" ordinal="NO|YES"

is an element to contain a variable definition. For example,

```
<COLUMN name="title">
```

Requirement: At least one COLUMN element is required.

COLUMN has these attributes:

name="*name*"
> specifies the name for the variable. The name must be a valid SAS name, which can be up to 32 characters.

> **Requirement:** The name= attribute is required.

retain="NO | YES"
> is an optional attribute that determines the contents of the input buffer at the beginning of each observation.

> NO
> > sets the value for the beginning of each observation either to MISSING or to the value of the DEFAULT element if specified. NO is the default.

> YES
> > keeps the current value until it is replaced by a new, non-missing value. Specifying YES is much like the RETAIN statement in DATA step processing. It forces the retention of processed values after an observation is written to the output data set.

> **Default:** The default is NO.

> **Featured in:** "Importing Hierarchical Data as Related Data Sets" on page 55.

ordinal="NO | YES"
> is an optional attribute that determines whether the variable is a counter variable (similar to the _N_ automatic variable in SAS DATA step processing) that keeps track of the number of times the location path, which is specified by the INCREMENT-PATH element, is encountered. The counter variable increments its count by 1 each time the path is matched. Counters can be useful for identifying individual occurrences of like-named data elements or for counting observations. The value for the ordinal= attribute also determines which column location path to use for collecting the column's values.

> NO
> > determines that the variable is not a counter variable, requires the PATH element, and does not allow INCREMENT-PATH and RESET-PATH elements. NO is the default.

> YES
> > determines that the variable is a counter variable, requires the INCREMENT-PATH element with the RESET-PATH element optional, and does not allow the PATH element.

> **Default:** NO

> **Featured in:** "Including a Key Field with Generated Numeric Keys" on page 58.

COLUMN can contain one or more of the following elements that describe the variable attributes: DATATYPE, DEFAULT, ENUM, FORMAT, INFORMAT, DESCRIPTION, LENGTH, TYPE, PATH, INCREMENT-PATH, and RESET-PATH.

TYPE

specifies the SAS data type (character or numeric) for the variable, which is how SAS stores the data. For example, the following specifies that the SAS data type for the variable is numeric:

```
<TYPE> numeric </TYPE>
```

Requirement: The TYPE element is required.

Tip: To assign a floating-point type, use

```
<DATATYPE> FLOAT </DATATYPE>
<TYPE> numeric </TYPE>
```

Tip: To apply output formatting, use the FORMAT element.

Tip: To control data type conversion on input, use the INFORMAT element.

```
<INFORMAT> datetime </INFORMAT>
```

DATATYPE

specifies the type of data being read from the XML document for the variable. For example, the following DATATYPE element specifies that the data contains alphanumeric characters:

```
<DATATYPE> string </DATATYPE>
```

The type of data specification can be

string

specifies that the data contains alphanumeric characters and does not contain numbers used for calculations.

integer

specifies that the data contains whole numbers used for calculations.

double

specifies that the data contains floating-point numbers.

dateTime

specifies that the input represents a valid datetime value, which is either

□ in the form of the XML specification ISO-8601 format. The default form is: `yyyy-mm-ddThh:mm:ss[.nnnnnn]`.

□ in a form for which a SAS informat (either supplied by SAS or user-written) properly translates the input into a valid SAS datetime value. See also the INFORMAT element.

date

specifies that the input represents a valid date value, which is either

□ in the form of the XML specification ISO-8601 format. The default form is: `yyyy-mm-dd`.

□ in a form for which a SAS informat (either supplied by SAS or user-written) properly translates the input into a valid SAS date value. See also the INFORMAT element.

time

specifies that the input represents a valid time value, which is either

□ in the form of the XML specification ISO-8601 format. The default form is: `hh:mm:ss[.nnnnnn]`.

□ in a form for which a SAS informat (either supplied by SAS or user-written) properly translates the input into a valid SAS date value. See also the INFORMAT element.

Requirement: The DATATYPE element is required.

Restriction: The values for XMLMap syntax Version 1.0 and 1.1 are not accepted by Version 1.2.

DEFAULT

is an optional element that specifies a default value for a missing value for the variable. Use the DEFAULT element in order to assign a non-missing value to missing data. For example, by including the following element, the engine will assign the value **single** when a missing value occurs:

```
<DEFAULT> single </DEFAULT>
```

Default: By default, the XML engine sets a missing value to MISSING.

Featured in: "Determining the Observation Boundary to Select the Best Columns" on page 64.

ENUM

is an optional element to contain a list of valid values for the variable. The ENUM element can contain one or more VALUE elements in order to list the values. By using ENUM, values in the XML document are verified against the list of values. If a value is not valid, then it is either set to MISSING (by default) or set to the value specified by the DEFAULT element. Note that a value specified for DEFAULT must be one of the ENUM values in order to be valid.

```
<COLUMN name="filing-status">
    .
    .
    .
    <DEFAULT> single </DEFAULT>
    .
    .
    .
    <ENUM>
        <VALUE> single </VALUE>
        <VALUE> married filing joint return </VALUE>
        <VALUE> married filing separate return </VALUE>
        <VALUE> head of household </VALUE>
        <VALUE> qualifying widow(er) </VALUE>
    </ENUM>
</COLUMN>
```

Featured in: "Determining the Observation Boundary to Select the Best Columns" on page 64.

FORMAT width="*w*" ndec="*d*"

is an optional element that specifies a SAS format for the variable. A format name can be up to 31 characters for a character format and 32 characters for a numeric format. A SAS format is an instruction that SAS uses to write values. You use formats to control the written appearance of values. Do not include a period (.) as part of the format name. Specify a width and length as attributes, not as part of the format name.

For a list of the SAS formats, see *SAS Language Reference: Dictionary*. For information on the ISO 8601 SAS formats, see Appendix 1, "ISO 8601 SAS Formats and Informats," on page 113.

Featured in: "Determining the Observation Boundary to Select the Best Columns" on page 64.

FORMAT has these attributes:

width="*w*"
> is an optional attribute that specifies a format width, which for most formats is the number of columns in the output data.

ndec="*d*"
> is an optional attribute that specifies a decimal scaling factor for numeric formats.

Here is an example:

```
<FORMAT> IS8601DA </FORMAT>
<FORMAT width="8"> best </FORMAT>
<FORMAT width="8" ndec="2"> dollar </FORMAT>
```

INFORMAT width="*w*" ndec="*d*"
> is an optional element that specifies a SAS informat for the variable. An informat name can be up to 30 characters for a character informat and 31 characters for a numeric informat. A SAS informat is an instruction that SAS uses to read values into a variable, that is, to store the values. Do not include a period (.) as part of the informat name. Specify a width and length as attributes, not as part of the informat name.
>
> For a list of the SAS informats, see *SAS Language Reference: Dictionary*. For information on the ISO 8601 SAS informats, see Appendix 1, "ISO 8601 SAS Formats and Informats," on page 113.

Featured in: "Determining the Observation Boundary to Select the Best Columns" on page 64.

INFORMAT has these attributes:

width="*w*"
> is an optional attribute that specifies an informat width, which for most informats is the number of columns in the input data.

ndec="*d*"
> is an optional attribute that specifies a decimal scaling factor for numeric informats. SAS divides the input data by 10 to the power of this value.

Here is an example:

```
<INFORMAT> IS8601DA </INFORMAT>
<INFORMAT width="8"> best </INFORMAT>
<INFORMAT width="8" ndec="2"> dollar </INFORMAT>
```

DESCRIPTION
> is an optional element that specifies a description for the variable, which can be up to 256 characters. The description is assigned as the variable label. For example,

```
<DESCRIPTION> Story link </DESCRIPTION>
```

LENGTH
> for character data, is the maximum field storage length from the XML data for the variable. The value refers to the number of bytes used to store each of the variable's values in a SAS data set. The value can be 1 to 32,767. During the input process, a maximum length of characters is read from the XML document and transferred to the observation buffer. For example,

```
<LENGTH> 200 </LENGTH>
```

Requirement: For data that is defined as a STRING data type, the LENGTH element is required.

Tip: You can use LENGTH to truncate a long field.

PATH syntax="*type*"
specifies a location path that tells the XML engine where in the XML document to locate and access a specific tag for the current variable, then perform a function as determined by the location path form in order to retrieve the value for the variable. The XPath forms that are supported allow elements and attributes to be individually selected for inclusion in the generated SAS data set.

Requirement: Whether the PATH element is required or not allowed is determined by the ordinal= attribute for the COLUMN element: if `ordinal="NO"`, which is the default, PATH is required and INCREMENT-PATH and RESET-PATH are not allowed; if `ordinal="YES"`, PATH is not allowed and INCREMENT-PATH is required, with RESET-PATH optional.

PATH has this attribute:

syntax="*type*"
is an optional attribute that specifies the type of syntax used to specify the location path. For Version 1.2, the syntax is a valid XPath construction in compliance with the World Wide Web Consortium (W3C). The XPath form supported by the XML engine allows elements and attributes to be individually selected for inclusion in the generated data set.

Default: The default is XPath, that is, `syntax="xpath"`.

Requirement: The XPath construction is a formal specification that puts a path description similar to UNIX on each element of the XML structure. *Note that XPath syntax is case sensitive. For example, if an element tag name is uppercase, it must be uppercase in the location path; if it is lowercase, it must be lowercase.* All paths must begin with the root-enclosing element (denoted by a slash '/') or with the "any parent" variant (denoted by double slashes '//'). Other W3C documented forms are not currently supported.

To specify the PATH location path, use one of the following forms.

CAUTION:
These forms are the only XPath forms that the XML engine supports. If you use any other valid W3C form, the results will be unpredictable. △

element-form
accesses PCDATA (parsable character data) from the named element.

```
<PATH syntax="xpath"> /rss/channel/title </PATH>
```

The above example tells the XML engine to scan the XML markup until it finds the specific TITLE element. The engine retrieves the value between the <TITLE> start tag and the </TITLE> end tag. That is, for the TITLE variable in the CHANNEL data set, the XML engine retrieves the highlighted value in the following XML document:

```
<?xml version="1.0" encoding="ISO-8859-1" ?>
<rss version="0.91">
   <channel>
```

```
<title>WriteTheWeb</title>
<link>http://writetheweb.com</link>
<description>News for web users that write back
    </description>
<language>en-us</language>
<copyright>Copyright 2000, WriteTheWeb team.
    </copyright>
<managingEditor>editor@writetheweb.com
    </managingEditor>
<webMaster>webmaster@writetheweb.com</webMaster>
<image>
    <title>WriteTheWeb</title>
    <url>http://writetheweb.com/images/mynetscape88.gif
        </url>
    <link>http://writetheweb.com</link>
    <width>88</width>
    <height>31</height>
    <description>News for web users that write back
        </description>
    </image>
<item>

        .
        .
        .

    </channel>
</rss>
```

attribute-form
accesses data from the named attribute (of the form **NAME="value"**).

```
<PATH syntax="xpath"> /rss@version </PATH>
```

The above example tells the XML engine to scan the XML markup until it finds the specific RSS element. The engine retrieves the value from the version= attribute in the RSS element. That is, for the VERSION variable in the CHANNEL data set, the XML engine would retrieve the highlighted value in the following XML document:

```
<?xml version="1.0" encoding="ISO-8859-1" ?>
<rss version="0.91">
    <channel>
        <title>WriteTheWeb</title>
        <link>http://writetheweb.com</link>
        <description>News for web users that write back
            </description>
        <language>en-us</language>
        <copyright>Copyright 2000, WriteTheWeb team.
            </copyright>
        <managingEditor>editor@writetheweb.com
            </managingEditor>
        <webMaster>webmaster@writetheweb.com</webMaster>
        <image>
            <title>WriteTheWeb</title>
            <url>http://writetheweb.com/images/mynetscape88.gif
                </url>
```

```
            <link>http://writetheweb.com</link>
            <width>88</width>
            <height>31</height>
            <description>News for web users that write back
               </description>
            </image>
         <item>
                  .

                  .

                  .
      </channel>
   </rss>
```

element-conditional-form
   accesses PCDATA from the named element with a specific attribute value.

```
<PATH syntax="xpath"> /constant[@name="PI"] </PATH>
```

If the XML contains the following, the above example tells the XML engine to
scan the XML markup until it finds the specific CONSTANT element where
the value of the name= attribute is PI. The engine would retrieve the value
3.14159.

```
<constant name="PI"> 3.14159 </constant>
```

INCREMENT-PATH syntax="*type*" beginend="Begin | End"
   specifies a location path for a counter variable, which is established by specifying
   the COLUMN element attribute **ordinal="YES"**. The location path tells the XML
   engine where in the XML document to increment the accumulated value for the
   counter variable by 1. The counter variable keeps track of the number of times a
   given path condition is met, which is applied to, for example, counting rows,
   multiple occurrences of data fields, or assignment of incremental key values.

Requirement: Whether the INCREMENT-PATH element is required or not
   allowed is determined by the ordinal= attribute for the COLUMN element: if
   ordinal="NO", which is the default, PATH is required and INCREMENT-PATH
   and RESET-PATH are not allowed; if **ordinal="YES"**, PATH is not allowed and
   INCREMENT-PATH is required with RESET-PATH optional.

Featured in: "Including a Key Field with Generated Numeric Keys" on page 58.

INCREMENT-PATH has these attributes:

syntax="*type*"
   is an optional attribute that specifies the type of syntax used to specify the
   location path. For Version 1.2, the syntax is a valid XPath construction in
   compliance with the World Wide Web Consortium (W3C). The XPath form
   supported by the XML engine allows elements and attributes to be
   individually selected for inclusion in the generated SAS data set.

Default: The default is XPath, that is, **syntax="xpath"**.

Requirement: The XPath construction is a formal specification that puts a
   path description similar to UNIX on each element of the XML structure.
   *Note that XPath syntax is case sensitive. For example, if an element tag
   name is uppercase, it must be uppercase in the location path; if it is
   lowercase, it must be lowercase.* All paths must begin with the
   root-enclosing element (denoted by a slash '/') or with the "any parent"
   variant (denoted by double slashes '//'). Other W3C documented forms are
   not currently supported.

beginend="Begin | End"
    is an optional attribute that specifies to stop processing when either the element start tag is encountered or the element end tag is encountered.
    Default: The default is Begin.

RESET-PATH syntax="*type*" beginend="Begin | End"
    specifies a location path for a counter variable, which is established by specifying the COLUMN element attribute `ordinal="YES"`. The location path tells the XML engine where in the XML document to reset the accumulated value for the counter variable to 0. The counter variable keeps track of the number of times a given path condition is met, which is applied to, for example, counting rows, multiple occurrences of data fields, or assignment of incremental key values.

Requirement: Whether the RESET-PATH element is optional or not allowed is determined by the ordinal= attribute for the COLUMN element: if `ordinal="NO"`, which is the default, PATH is required and INCREMENT-PATH and RESET-PATH are not allowed; if `ordinal="YES"`, PATH is not allowed and INCREMENT-PATH is required with RESET-PATH optional. RESET-PATH is always an optional element.

RESET-PATH has these attributes:

syntax="*type*"
    is an optional attribute that specifies the type of syntax used to specify the location path. For Version 1.2, the syntax is a valid XPath construction in compliance with the World Wide Web Consortium (W3C). The XPath form supported by the XML engine allows elements and attributes to be individually selected for inclusion in the generated SAS data set.
    Default: The default is XPath, that is, `syntax="xpath"`.
    Requirement: The XPath construction is a formal specification that puts a UNIX-like path description on each element of the XML structure. *Note that XPath syntax is case sensitive. For example, if an element tag name is uppercase, it must be uppercase in the location path; if it is lowercase, it must be lowercase.* All paths must begin with the root-enclosing element (denoted by a slash '/') or with the "any parent" variant (denoted by double slashes '//'). Other W3C documented forms are not currently supported.

beginend="Begin | End"
    is an optional attribute that specifies to stop processing when either the element start tag is encountered or the element end tag is encountered.
    Default: The default is Begin.

Using SAS XML Mapper to Generate and Update an XMLMap

What Is SAS XML Mapper?

SAS XML Mapper is a Java-based application that assists you in creating and modifying XMLMaps for use by the XML engine.

SAS XML Mapper provides a graphical interface that you can use in order to generate the appropriate XML elements. SAS XML Mapper analyzes the structure of an XML document or an XML schema and generates basic XML syntax for the XMLMap.

The interface consists of windows, a menu bar, and a tool bar. Using SAS XML Mapper, you can display an XML document or an XML schema, create and modify an XMLMap, and generate example SAS programs.

Display 8.1   SAS XML Mapper

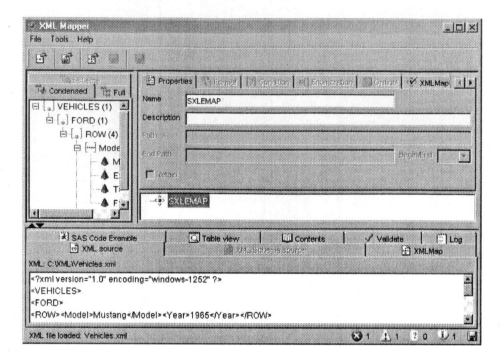

Using the Windows

The XML window and the XMLMap window are the two primary windows. The XML window, which is on the left, displays an XML document in a tree structure. The XMLMap window, which is on the right, displays an XMLMap in a tree structure. The map tree displays three layers: the top level is the map itself, the second tier includes tables, and the leaf nodes are columns. The detail area at the top displays information about the currently selected item, such as attributes for the table or column. The information is subdivided into tabs.

There are several source windows on the bottom of the interface, such as the XML source window, the XMLMap source window, the SAS code example window, and so on.

Using the Menu Bar

The menu bar provides pull-down menus in order to request functionality. For example, select the **File** menu, then **Open XML** in order to display a browser so that you can select an XML document to open.

Using the Tool Bar

The tool bar contains icons for shortcuts to several items on the menu bar. For example, the first icon from the left is the **Open an XML file** icon. Select it in order to display a browser to so that you can select an XML document to open.

How Do I Get SAS XML Mapper?

SAS XML Mapper is available for installation from your SAS Installation Kit. SAS XML Mapper is on the SAS Client-Side Components Volume 1 CD.

SAS XML Mapper has online help attached, which includes a usage example. From the menu bar, select **Help**, then **Help Topics**.

Using XMLMap Manager to Manage XMLMaps as Metadata Objects

What Is XMLMap Manager?

XMLMap Manager provides centralized management of XMLMaps as metadata objects in a SAS metadata environment. You can use XMLMap Manager to

☐ import existing XMLMaps and store them as metadata objects

☐ create new XMLMaps by invoking SAS XML Mapper

☐ manage your XMLMaps.

Display 8.2 XMLMap Manager

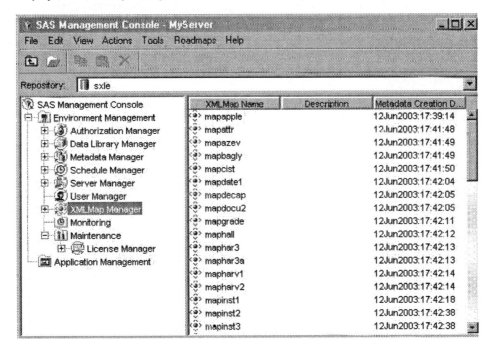

How Do I Get XMLMap Manager?

XMLMap Manager is a plug-in on the SAS Management Console, which is available for installation from your SAS Installation Kit. SAS Management Console is on the SAS Client-Side Components Volume 1 CD.

From the SAS Management Console, the XMLMap Manager plug-in is available from **Environment Management**.

To display online help, select **XMLMap Manager**, then from the menu bar, select **Help**, then **Help on XMLMap Manager**.

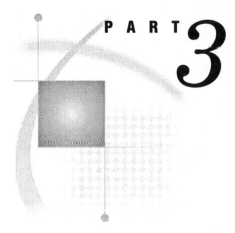

PART 3

Appendixes

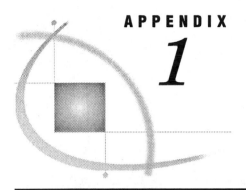

ISO 8601 SAS Formats and Informats

SAS Support of the ISO 8601 Standard

Introduction

ISO 8601 is an international standard for the representation of dates and times. The standard defines a large number of alternative representations of dates, times, and time intervals.

The representations can be either in a *basic format* that has a minimal number of characters or in an *extended format* that adds characters to enhance human readability. For example, January 3, 2003 can be represented as either 20030103 (basic format) or 2003-01-03 (extended format).

The SAS XML LIBNAME engine supports ISO 8601 date and time representations with several SAS formats and SAS informats.

Elements of the ISO 8601 Standard Not Supported

SAS does not support or does not fully support the ISO 8601 elements listed in the following table:

Table A1.1   Elements of the ISO 8601 Standard Not Supported or Not Fully Supported

Element		Category
5.2.1.2	Representations with reduced precision	Date
5.2.1.3	Truncated representations	Date
5.2.1.4	Expanded representations	Date
5.2.2	Ordinal date	Date
5.2.3	Week date	Date
5.3.1.2	Representations with reduced precision	Time
5.3.1.3	Representation of decimal fractions	Time
	Fractions are supported only on the seconds field value and use a decimal point delimiter.	
5.3.1.4	Truncated representations	Time
5.3.1.5	Representation with time designator	Time
5.3.2	Midnight	Time
	Only the zero hour representation is supported.	
5.3.3	Coordinated Universal Time (UTC)	Time
	Only full *hhmmss* forms in either extended or basic format can contain the UTC designator.	
5.3.4.1	Difference between local time and Coordinated Universal Time	Time
5.3.4.2	Local time and the difference with Coordinated Universal Time	Time

Element		Category
5.4.1	Complete representation	Datetime
	Only subitem a) For calendar dates is supported. Subitems b) For ordinal dates and c) For week dates are not supported.	
5.4.2	Representations other than complete	Datetime
5.5	Time-intervals	Time
5.6	Recurring time-intervals	Time

Understanding Time Zone Processing

The SAS formats and informats that support the ISO 8601 standard read and write time values with and without a time zone indicator. There are specific formats and informats for time zone sensitive and time zone insensitive processing. Note that using a time zone indicator with a time zone insensitive informat or not using a time zone indicator with a time zone sensitive informat is considered an error.

Without a time zone indicator, the context of the value is local time. That is, the value is assumed to be in some local time zone and no conversion or adjustment is made. For example, in the United States in the state of Texas, the value 09:00:00 is 9:00 a.m. Central Standard Time and in the state of North Carolina, the value is 9:00 a.m. Eastern Standard Time. Note that these time values are not equivalent to Coordinated Universal Time (UTC) time values due to the differing time zones.

With a time zone offset present, time zone sensitive informats convert the value to UTC, which is the international time standard. For example, the value 09:00:00-05:00 is converted to 15:00:00, which is 3:00 p.m. With the Z time zone indicator (a special case in the ISO standard), the value is assumed to be expressed in UTC and no adjustment or conversion is made.

CAUTION:
> **With all time informats, the time zone context is not stored with the value. It is recommended that you do not mix time-based values.** When a time value is read into a variable using a time zone sensitive SAS informat, the value is adjusted to UTC as requested via the time zone indicator, but the time zone context is not stored with the value. When a time value is written using a time zone sensitive SAS format, the value is expressed as UTC with a zero offset value and is not adjusted to or from local time. △

See the example "Importing Time Values with a Time Zone" on page 126.

SAS Informats for the Extended Format

Introduction

This set of SAS informats represents the ISO 8601 extended format. Each informat has a corresponding SAS format that represents the extended format.

IS8601DA Informat

Syntax: IS8601DA
Category: Date
ISO 8601 Element: 5.2.1.1 Complete representation
The IS8601DA informat reads date values into a variable in the extended format
YYYY-MM-DD, where

YYYY
    is a four-digit year including century, for example, 2003.

MM
    is a two-digit month (zero padded), for example, 01 is January.

DD
    is a two-digit day of the month (zero padded), that is, 01 through 31.

IS8601DN Informat

Syntax: IS8601DN
Category: Datetime
Time Zone: No
ISO 8601 Element: 5.2.1.1 Complete representation
The IS8601DN informat reads datetime values with only a date portion into a
variable in the extended format *YYYY-MM-DD*, where

YYYY
    is a four-digit year including century, for example, 2003.

MM
    is a two-digit month (zero padded), for example, 01 is January.

DD
    is a two-digit day of the month (zero padded), that is, 01 through 31.

IS8601DT Informat

Syntax: IS8601DT
Category: Datetime
Time Zone: No
ISO 8601 Element: 5.4.1 Complete representation
The IS8601DT informat reads datetime values into a variable in the extended format
YYYY-MM-DDThh:mm:ss[.fffff], where

YYYY
    is a four-digit year including century, for example, 2003.

MM
    is a two-digit month (zero padded), for example, 01 is January.

DD
    is a two-digit day of the month (zero padded), that is, 01 through 31.

T
    is a required capital letter T to indicate the beginning of the time element.

hh
    is a two-digit hour (zero padded), that is, 00 through 23.

mm

is a two-digit minute (zero padded), that is, 00 through 59.

ss

is a two-digit second (zero padded), that is, 00 through 59.

.fffff

are optional fractional seconds.

IS8601DZ Informat

Syntax: IS8601DZ
Category: Datetime
Time Zone: Yes
ISO 8601 Element: 5.4.1 Complete representation
The IS8601DZ informat reads datetime values with a time zone into a variable in the extended format *YYYY-MM-DDThh:mm:ss[.fffff][Z] | [[+ | -]hh:mm]*, where

YYYY

is a four-digit year including century, for example, 2003.

MM

is a two-digit month (zero padded), for example, 01 is January.

DD

is a two-digit day of the month (zero padded), that is, 01 through 31.

T

is a required capital letter T to indicate the beginning of the time element.

hh

is a two-digit hour (zero padded), that is, 00 through 23.

mm

is a two-digit minute (zero padded), that is, 00 through 59.

ss

is a two-digit second (zero padded), that is, 00 through 59.

.fffff

are optional fractional seconds.

Z

is an optional capital letter Z to indicate Universal Coordinated Time.

+ | -hh:mm

is an optional hour and minute signed offset from UTC base. Note that the offset must be *+ | -hh:mm* (that is, + or - and five characters). The shorter form *+ | -hh* is not supported.

IS8601LZ Informat

Syntax: IS8601LZ
Category: Time
Time Zone: Yes
ISO 8601 Element: 5.3.1.1 Complete representation
The IS8601LZ informat reads time values with a time zone into a variable in the extended format *hh:mm:ss[.fffff][Z][[+ | -]hh:mm]*, where

hh
> is a two-digit hour (zero padded), that is, 00 through 23.

mm
> is a two-digit minute (zero padded), that is, 00 through 59.

ss
> is a two-digit second (zero padded), that is, 00 through 59.

.fffff
> are optional fractional seconds.

Z
> is an optional capital letter Z to indicate Universal Coordinated Time.

+|-hh:mm
> is an optional hour and minute signed offset from UTC base. Note that the offset must be *+|-hh:mm* (that is, + or - and five characters). The shorter form *+|-hh* is not supported.

IS8601TM Informat

Syntax: IS8601TM
Category: Time
Time Zone: No
ISO 8601 Element: 5.3.1.1 Complete representation and 5.3.1.3 Representation of decimal fractions
The IS8601TM informat reads time values into a variable in the extended format *hh:mm:ss[.fffff]*, where

hh
> is a two-digit hour (zero padded), that is, 00 through 23.

mm
> is a two-digit minute (zero padded), that is, 00 through 59.

ss
> is a two-digit second (zero padded), that is, 00 through 59.

.fffff
> are optional fractional seconds.

IS8601TZ Informat

Syntax: IS8601TZ
Category: Time
Time Zone: Yes
ISO 8601 Element: 5.3.1.1 Complete representation
The IS8601TZ informat reads time values with a time zone into a variable in the extended format *hh:mm:ss[.fffff][Z][[+|-]hh:mm]*, where

hh
> is a two-digit hour (zero padded), that is, 00 through 23.

mm
> is a two-digit minute (zero padded), that is, 00 through 59.

ss
> is a two-digit second (zero padded), that is, 00 through 59.

.fffff
> are optional fractional seconds.

Z
> is an optional capital letter Z to indicate Universal Coordinated Time.

+|-*hh:mm*
> is an optional hour and minute signed offset from UTC base. Note that the offset must be +|-*hh:mm* (that is, + or - and five characters). The shorter form +|-*hh* is not supported.

SAS Informats for the Basic Format

Introduction

This set of SAS informats represents the ISO 8601 basic format. The ND part of the informat's syntax designates non-delimited.

Note: Because using the basic format in XML content is discouraged, it is recommended that when you read in values with one of the basic format SAS informats, you write values with the corresponding extended format SAS format. △

ND8601DA Informat

Syntax: ND8601DA
Category: Date
ISO 8601 Element: 5.2.1.1 Complete representation
The ND8601DA informat reads date values into a variable in the basic format *YYYYMMDD*, where

YYYY
> is a four-digit year including century, for example, 2003.

MM
> is a two-digit month (zero padded), for example, 01 is January.

DD
> is a two-digit day of the month (zero padded), that is, 01 through 31.

ND8601DN Informat

Syntax: ND8601DN
Category: Datetime
Time Zone: No
ISO 8601 Element: 5.2.1.1 Complete representation
The ND8601DN informat reads datetime values with only a date portion into a variable in the basic format *YYYYMMDD*, where

YYYY
> is a four-digit year including century, for example, 2003.

MM
> is a two-digit month (zero padded), for example, 01 is January.

DD

is a two-digit day of the month (zero padded), that is, 01 through 31.

ND8601DT Informat

Syntax: ND8601DT
Category: Datetime
Time Zone: No
ISO 8601 Element: 5.4.1 Complete representation
The ND8601DT informat reads datetime values into a variable in the basic format
YYYYMMDDhhmmss.[fffff], where

YYYY

is a four-digit year including century, for example, 2003.

MM

is a two-digit month (zero padded), for example, 01 is January.

DD

is a two-digit day of the month (zero padded), that is, 01 through 31.

hh

is a two-digit hour (zero padded), that is, 00 through 23.

mm

is a two-digit minute (zero padded), that is, 00 through 59.

ss

is a two-digit second (zero padded), that is, 00 through 59.

.fffff

are optional fractional seconds.

ND8601DZ Informat

Syntax: ND8601DZ
Category: Datetime
Time Zone: Yes
ISO 8601 Element: 5.4.1 Complete representation
The ND8601DZ informat reads datetime values with a time zone into a variable in
the basic format *YYYYMMDDhhmmss[.fffff][[+|-]hhmm]*, where

YYYY

is a four-digit year (zero padded), for example, 2003.

MM

is a two-digit month (zero padded), for example, 01 is January.

DD

is a two-digit day of the month (zero padded), that is, 01 through 31.

hh

is a two-digit hour (zero padded), that is, 00 through 23.

mm

is a two-digit minute (zero padded), that is, 00 through 59.

ss

is a two-digit second (zero padded), that is, 00 through 59.

.fffff
    are optional fractional seconds.

+|-hhmm
    is an optional hour and minute signed offset from UTC base. Note that the offset must be *+|-hhmm* (that is, + or - and four characters). The shorter form *+|-hh* is not supported.

ND8601TM Informat

Syntax: ND8601TM
Category: Time
Time Zone: No
ISO 8601 Element: 5.3.1.1 Complete representation and 5.3.1.3 Representation of decimal fractions
The ND8601TM informat reads time values into a variable in the basic format *hhmmss*, where

hh
    is a two-digit hour (zero padded), that is, 00 through 23.

mm
    is a two-digit minute (zero padded), that is, 00 through 59.

ss
    is a two-digit second (zero padded), that is, 00 through 59.

ND8601TZ Informat

Syntax: ND8601TZ
Category: Time
Time Zone: Yes
ISO 8601 Element: 5.3.1.1 Complete representation
The ND8601TZ informat reads time values with a time zone into a variable in the basic format *hhmmss*⌊*.fffff*⌋⌊*+|-*⌋*hhmm*⌋, where

hh
    is a two-digit hour (zero padded), that is, 00 through 23.

mm
    is a two-digit minute (zero padded), that is, 00 through 59.

ss
    is a two-digit second (zero padded), that is, 00 through 59.

.fffff
    are optional fractional seconds.

+|-hhmm
    is an optional hour and minute signed offset from UTC base. Note that the offset must be *+|-hhmm* (that is, + or - and four characters). The shorter form *+|-hh* is not supported.

SAS Formats for the Extended Format

Introduction

This set of SAS formats represents the ISO 8601 extended format. Each SAS format has a corresponding SAS informat that represents the extended format.

IS8601DA Format

Syntax: IS8601DA
Category: Date
ISO 8601 Element: 5.2.1.1 Complete representation
The IS8601DA format writes data values in the extended format *YYYY-MM-DD*, where

YYYY
> is a four-digit year including century, for example, 2003.

MM
> is a two-digit month (zero padded), for example, 01 is January.

DD
> is a two-digit day of the month (zero padded), that is, 01 through 31.

IS8601DN Format

Syntax: IS8601DN
Category: Datetime
Time Zone: No
ISO 8601 Element: 5.2.1.1 Complete representation
The IS8601DN format writes datetime values with only a date portion in the extended format *YYYY-MM-DD*, where

YYYY
> is a four-digit year including century, for example, 2003.

MM
> is a two-digit month (zero padded), for example, 01 is January.

DD
> is a two-digit day of the month (zero padded), that is, 01 through 31.

IS8601DT Format

Syntax: IS8601DT
Category: Datetime
Time Zone: No
ISO 8601 Element: 5.4.1 Complete representation
The IS8601DT format writes datetime values in the extended format *YYYY-MM-DDThh:mm:ss[.fffff]*, where

YYYY
> is a four-digit year including century, for example, 2003.

MM
   is a two-digit month (zero padded), for example, 01 is January.

DD
   is a two-digit day of the month (zero padded), that is, 01 through 31.

T
   is a required capital letter T to indicate the beginning of the time element.

hh
   is a two-digit hour (zero padded), that is, 00 through 23.

mm
   is a two-digit minute (zero padded), that is, 00 through 59.

ss
   is a two-digit second (zero padded), that is, 00 through 59.

.fffff
   are optional fractional seconds.

IS8601DZ Format

Syntax: IS8601DZ
Category: Datetime
Time Zone: Yes
ISO 8601 Element: 5.4.1 Complete representation
The IS8601DZ format writes datetime values with a time zone in the extended
format *YYYY-MM-DDThh:mm:ss*[*.fffff*][Z] | [[+|-]*hh:mm*], where

YYYY
   is a four-digit year including century, for example, 2003.

MM
   is a two-digit month (zero padded), for example, 01 is January.

DD
   is a two-digit day of the month (zero padded), that is, 01 through 31.

T
   is a required capital letter T to indicate the beginning of the time element.

hh
   is a two-digit hour (zero padded), that is, 00 through 23.

mm
   is a two-digit minute (zero padded), that is, 00 through 59.

ss
   is a two-digit second (zero padded), that is, 00 through 59.

.fffff
   are optional fractional seconds.

Z
   is an optional capital letter Z to indicate Universal Coordinated Time.

+|-*hh:mm*
   is an optional hour and minute signed offset from UTC base. Note that the offset
   must be +|-*hh:mm* (that is, + or - and five characters). The shorter form +|-*hh* is
   not supported.

IS8601LZ Format

Syntax: IS8601LZ
Category: Time
Time Zone: Yes. The format appends the UTC offset to the value as determined by the local SAS session.
ISO 8601 Element: 5.3.1.1 Complete representation
The IS8601LZ format writes time values with a time zone in the extended format *hh:mm:ss*[.*fffff*][Z][+|-]*hh:mm*], where

hh
    is a two-digit hour (zero padded), that is, 00 through 23.

mm
    is a two-digit minute (zero padded), that is, 00 through 59.

ss
    is a two-digit second (zero padded), that is, 00 through 59.

.fffff
    are optional fractional seconds.

Z
    is an optional capital letter Z to indicate Universal Coordinated Time.

+|-*hh:mm*
    is an optional hour and minute signed offset from UTC base. Note that the offset must be +|-*hh:mm* (that is, + or - and five characters). The shorter form +|-*hh* is not supported.

IS8601TM Format

Syntax: IS8601TM
Category: Time
Time Zone: No
ISO 8601 Element: 5.3.1.1 Complete representation and 5.3.1.3 Representation of decimal fractions
The IS8601TM format writes time values in the extended format *hh:mm:ss*[.*fffff*], where

hh
    is a two-digit hour (zero padded), that is, 00 through 23.

mm
    is a two-digit minute (zero padded), that is, 00 through 59.

ss
    is a two-digit second (zero padded), that is, 00 through 59.

.fffff
    are optional fractional seconds.

IS8601TZ Format

Syntax: IS8601TZ
Category: Time
Time Zone: Yes

ISO 8601 Element: 5.3.1.1 Complete representation

The IS8601TZ format writes time values with a time zone in the extended format *hh:mm:ss*[*.fffff*][Z][+|-]*hh:mm*], where

hh

is a two-digit hour (zero padded), that is, 00 through 23.

mm

is a two-digit minute (zero padded), that is, 00 through 59.

ss

is a two-digit second (zero padded), that is, 00 through 59.

.fffff

are optional fractional seconds.

Z

is an optional capital letter Z to indicate Universal Coordinated Time.

+|-*hh:mm*

is an optional hour and minute signed offset from UTC base. Note that the offset must be +|-*hh:mm* (that is, + or - and five characters). The shorter form +|-*hh* is not supported.

Using the Informats and Formats

Importing Both Basic Format and Extended Format Dates

This simple example illustrates importing an XML document that contains date values in both the basic format and the extended format. The XMLMap uses the FORMAT and INFORMAT elements to specify the appropriate SAS format and SAS informat in order to represent the dates according to ISO 8601 standards.

First, here is the XML document:

```
<?xml version="1.0" ?>
<Root>
  <ISODATE>
    <BASIC>20010911</BASIC>
    <EXTENDED>2001-09-11</EXTENDED>
  </ISODATE>
</Root>
```

The following XMLMap imports the XML document using the SAS informats and formats to read and write the date values:

```
<?xml version="1.0" encoding="UTF-8"?>
<SXLEMAP version="1.2" name="ISOdate"
    description="Reading a Basic and Extended format ISO date field">
  <!-- ####################################################### -->
  <TABLE name="ISODATE">
    <TABLE-PATH syntax="XPath">/Root/ISODATE</TABLE-PATH>

    <COLUMN name="BASIC">
      <PATH  syntax="XPath">/Root/ISODATE/BASIC</PATH>
      <TYPE>numeric</TYPE>
      <DATATYPE>date</DATATYPE>
```

```
<FORMAT width="10">IS8601DA</FORMAT>  ❶
<INFORMAT width="8">ND8601DA</INFORMAT>  ❷
</COLUMN>

<COLUMN name="EXTENDED">
  <PATH  syntax="XPath">/Root/ISODATE/EXTENDED</PATH>
  <TYPE>numeric</TYPE>
  <DATATYPE>date</DATATYPE>
  <FORMAT>IS8601DA</FORMAT>  ❸
  <INFORMAT>IS8601DA</INFORMAT>  ❹
</COLUMN>

</TABLE>

</SXLEMAP>
```

The following explains the XMLMap syntax that imports the date values:

1 For the Basic variable, the FORMAT element specifies the IS8601DA SAS format, which writes data values in the extended format *YYYY-MM-DD*.

2 For the Basic variable, the INFORMAT element specifies the ND8601DA SAS informat, which reads date values into a variable in the basic format *YYYYMMDD*.

   Note: As recommended, when you read values into a variable with a basic format SAS informat, this example writes the values with the corresponding extended format SAS format. △

3 For the Extended variable, the FORMAT element specifies the IS8601DA SAS format, which writes data values in the extended format *YYYY-MM-DD*.

4 For the Extended variable, the INFORMAT element specifies the IS8601DA SAS informat, which reads date values into a variable in the basic format *YYYY-MM-DD*.

The following SAS statements import the XML document and display PRINT procedure output:

```
filename dates 'c:\My Documents\XML\ISOdate.xml';
filename map 'c:\My Documents\XML\ISOdate.map';
libname dates xml xmlmap=map;

proc print data=dates.isodate;
run;
```

Output A1.1   PRINT Procedure Output for Imported Data Set DATES.ISODATE

```
            The SAS System                              1

       Obs     BASIC          EXTENDED

        1     2001-09-11     2001-09-11
```

Importing Time Values with a Time Zone

This example illustrates importing an XML document that contains time values in various forms. The XMLMap uses the FORMAT and INFORMAT elements to specify the appropriate SAS formats and SAS informats in order to represent the times appropriately.

First, here is an XML document that contains a variety of time values:

```
<?xml version="1.0" ?>
<Root>
   <TIME>
      <LOCAL>09:00:00</LOCAL>
      <UTC>09:00:00Z</UTC>
      <OFFSET>14:00:00+05:00</OFFSET>
   </TIME>
</Root>
```

The following XMLMap imports the XML document using the SAS informats and formats to read and write the time values:

```
<?xml version="1.0" encoding="UTF-8"?>
<SXLEMAP version="1.2" name="ISOtime">
     description="Reading time values with and without offsets">
   <!-- ###################################################### -->
   <TABLE name="TIME">
     <TABLE-PATH syntax="XPath">/Root/TIME</TABLE-PATH>

     <COLUMN name="LOCAL">
       <PATH  syntax="XPath">/Root/TIME/LOCAL</PATH>
       <TYPE>numeric</TYPE>
       <DATATYPE>time</DATATYPE>
       <INFORMAT width="8">IS8601TM</INFORMAT>  ❶
       <FORMAT width="8">IS8601TM</FORMAT>
          </COLUMN>

     <COLUMN name="LOCALZONE">
       <PATH  syntax="XPath">/Root/TIME/LOCAL</PATH>
       <TYPE>numeric</TYPE>
       <DATATYPE>time</DATATYPE>
       <INFORMAT width="8">IS8601TM</INFORMAT>  ❷
       <FORMAT width="14">IS8601LZ</FORMAT>
     </COLUMN>

     <COLUMN name="UTC">
       <PATH  syntax="XPath">/Root/TIME/UTC</PATH>
       <TYPE>numeric</TYPE>
       <DATATYPE>time</DATATYPE>
       <INFORMAT width="9">IS8601TZ</INFORMAT>  ❸
       <FORMAT width="9">IS8601TZ</FORMAT>
          </COLUMN>

     <COLUMN name="OFFSET">
       <PATH  syntax="XPath">/Root/TIME/OFFSET</PATH>
       <TYPE>numeric</TYPE>
       <DATATYPE>time</DATATYPE>
       <INFORMAT width="14">IS8601TZ</INFORMAT>  ❹
       <FORMAT width="14">IS8601TZ</FORMAT>
          </COLUMN>
   </TABLE>
```

```
</SXLEMAP>
```

The following explains the XMLMap syntax that imports the time values:

1 For the Local variable, the INFORMAT and FORMAT elements specify the *IS8601TM* SAS informat and format, which reads and writes time values in the extended format *hh:mm:ss*[.*fffff*]. Because there is no time zone indicator, the context of the value is local time.

2 For the Localzone variable, which reads the same value as the Local variable, the INFORMAT element specifies the *IS8601TM* SAS informat, which reads time values in the extended format *hh:mm:ss*[.*fffff*. Because there is no time zone indicator, the context of the value is local time.

   The FORMAT element, however, specifies the *IS8601LZ* SAS format, which writes time values in the extended format *hh:mm:ss*[.*fffff*][Z][+|-]*hh:mm*]. The IS8601LZ format appends the UTC offset to the value as determined by the local, current SAS session. Using the IS8601LZ format enables you to provide a time notation in order to eliminate the ambiguity of local time.

   Note: Even with the time notation, it is recommended that you do not mix time-based values. △

3 For the UTC variable, the INFORMAT and FORMAT elements specify the *IS8601TZ* SAS informat and format, which reads and writes time values in the extended format *hh:mm:ss*[.*fffff*][Z][+|-]*hh:mm*]. Because there is a time zone indicator, the value is assumed to be expressed in UTC. No adjustment or conversion is made to the value.

4 For the Offset variable, the INFORMAT and FORMAT elements specify the *IS8601TZ* SAS informat and format, which reads and writes time values in the extended format *hh:mm:ss*[.*fffff*][Z][+|-]*hh:mm*]. Because there is a time zone offset present, when the time value is read into the variable using the time zone sensitive SAS informat, the value is adjusted to UTC as requested via the time zone indicator, but the time zone context is not stored with the value. When the time value is written using the time zone sensitive SAS format, the value is expressed as UTC with a zero offset value and is not adjusted to or from local time.

The following SAS statements import the XML document and display the PRINT procedure output:

```
filename timzn 'c:\My Documents\XML\Time.xml';
filename map 'c:\My Documents\XML\Time.map';
libname timzn xml xmlmap=map;

proc print data=timzn.time;
run;
```

Output A1.2   PRINT Procedure Output for Imported Data Set TIMZN.TIME

```
                             The SAS System                              1

          Obs     LOCAL       LOCALZONE        UTC         OFFSET

           1     09:00:00    09:00:00-04:00  09:00:00Z   09:00:00+00:00
```

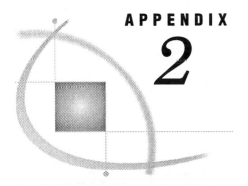

Sample XML Document

Example CDISC ODM Document

Here is an example of an XML document that is in CDISC ODM format. This file is used in "Importing a CDISC ODM Document" on page 39 and in "Exporting an XML Document in CDISC ODM Format" on page 27.

```
<?xml version="1.0" encoding="iso-8859-1" ?>
<!--
      Clinical Data Interchange Standards Consortium (CDISC)
      Operational Data Model (ODM) for clinical data interchange

      You can learn more about CDISC standards efforts at
      http://www.cdisc.org/standards/index.html
  -->

<ODM xmlns="http://www.cdisc.org/ns/odm/v1.2"
     xmlns:ds="http://www.w3.org/2000/09/xmldsig#"
     xmlns:xsi="http://www.w3.org/2001/XMLSchema-instance"
     xsi:schemaLocation="http://www.cdisc.org/ns/odm/v1.2 ODM1-2-0.xsd"

     ODMVersion="1.2"
     FileOID="000-00-0000"
     FileType="Snapshot"
     Description="Adverse events from the CTChicago file"

     AsOfDateTime="2004-04-14T18:09:09"
     CreationDateTime="2004-04-14T18:09:09"
     SourceSystem="SAS 9.1"
     SourceSystemVersion="9.01.01M0D11182003">

   <Study OID="STUDY.StudyOID">

     <!--
           GlobalVariables is a REQUIRED section in ODM markup.
       -->
     <GlobalVariables>
       <StudyName>CDISC Connect-A-Thon Test Study III</StudyName>
       <StudyDescription>This file contains test data for the
```

```
        CDISC Connect-A-Thon event scheduled for the DIA 38th annual
        meeting in Chicago.</StudyDescription>
        <ProtocolName>CDISC-Protocol-00-000</ProtocolName>
    </GlobalVariables>

    <BasicDefinitions />

    <!--
        Internal ODM markup required metadata
        This section is generated from the data records contained
        in the CLINICALDATA table(s). Each table becomes its own
        form definition.
    -->
    <MetaDataVersion OID="v1.1.0" Name="Version 1.1.0">
      <Protocol>
        <StudyEventRef StudyEventOID="SE.VISIT1" OrderNumber="1"
         Mandatory="Yes" />
      </Protocol>

      <StudyEventDef OID="SE.VISIT1" Name="Study Event Definition"
         Repeating="No" Type="Common">
        <FormRef FormOID="FORM.AE" OrderNumber="1" Mandatory="No" />
      </StudyEventDef>

      <FormDef OID="FORM.AE" Name="Form Definition" Repeating="No">
        <ItemGroupRef ItemGroupOID="IG.AE" Mandatory="No" />
      </FormDef>


      <!--
          Columns defined in the table
      -->
      <ItemGroupDef OID="IG.AE" Repeating="No"
                    SASDatasetName="AE"
                    Name="Adverse Events"
                    Domain="AE"
                    Comment="All adverse events in this trial">
        <ItemRef ItemOID="ID.TAREA" OrderNumber="1" Mandatory="No"/>
        <ItemRef ItemOID="ID.PNO" OrderNumber="2" Mandatory="No"/>
        <ItemRef ItemOID="ID.SCTRY" OrderNumber="3" Mandatory="No"/>
        <ItemRef ItemOID="ID.F_STATUS" OrderNumber="4" Mandatory="No"/>
        <ItemRef ItemOID="ID.LINE_NO" OrderNumber="5" Mandatory="No"/>
        <ItemRef ItemOID="ID.AETERM" OrderNumber="6" Mandatory="No"/>
        <ItemRef ItemOID="ID.AESTMON" OrderNumber="7" Mandatory="No"/>
        <ItemRef ItemOID="ID.AESTDAY" OrderNumber="8" Mandatory="No"/>
        <ItemRef ItemOID="ID.AESTYR" OrderNumber="9" Mandatory="No"/>
        <ItemRef ItemOID="ID.AESTDT" OrderNumber="10" Mandatory="No"/>
        <ItemRef ItemOID="ID.AEENMON" OrderNumber="11" Mandatory="No"/>
        <ItemRef ItemOID="ID.AEENDAY" OrderNumber="12" Mandatory="No"/>
        <ItemRef ItemOID="ID.AEENYR" OrderNumber="13" Mandatory="No"/>
        <ItemRef ItemOID="ID.AEENDT" OrderNumber="14" Mandatory="No"/>
        <ItemRef ItemOID="ID.AESEV" OrderNumber="15" Mandatory="No"/>
        <ItemRef ItemOID="ID.AEREL" OrderNumber="16" Mandatory="No"/>
        <ItemRef ItemOID="ID.AEOUT" OrderNumber="17" Mandatory="No"/>
```

```xml
        <ItemRef ItemOID="ID.AEACTTRT" OrderNumber="18" Mandatory="No/>
        <ItemRef ItemOID="ID.AECONTRT" OrderNumber="19" Mandatory="No"/>
    </ItemGroupDef>



    <!--
            Column attributes as defined in the table
        -->
<ItemDef OID="ID.TAREA" SASFieldName="TAREA" Name="Therapeutic Area"
    DataType="text" Length="4">
    <CodeListRef CodeListOID="CL.$TAREAF" />
</ItemDef>
<ItemDef OID="ID.PNO" SASFieldName="PNO" Name="Protocol Number"
    DataType="text" Length="15" />
<ItemDef OID="ID.SCTRY" SASFieldName="SCTRY" Name="Country"
    DataType="text" Length="4">
    <CodeListRef CodeListOID="CL.$SCTRYF" />
</ItemDef>
<ItemDef OID="ID.F_STATUS" SASFieldName="F_STATUS"
    Name="Record status, 5 levels, internal use" DataType="text"
    Length="1">
    <CodeListRef CodeListOID="CL.$F_STATU" />
</ItemDef>
<ItemDef OID="ID.LINE_NO" SASFieldName="LINE_NO" Name="Line Number"
    DataType="float" />
<ItemDef OID="ID.AETERM" SASFieldName="AETERM"
    Name="Conmed Indication" DataType="text" Length="100" />
<ItemDef OID="ID.AESTMON" SASFieldName="AESTMON"
    Name="Start Month - Enter Two Digits 01-12" DataType="text"
    Length="2" />
<ItemDef OID="ID.AESTDAY" SASFieldName="AESTDAY"
    Name="Start Day - Enter Two Digits 01-31" DataType="text"
    Length="2" />
<ItemDef OID="ID.AESTYR" SASFieldName="AESTYR"
    Name="Start Year - Enter Four Digit Year" DataType="text"
    Length="4" />
<ItemDef OID="ID.AESTDT" SASFieldName="AESTDT"
    Name="Derived Start Date" DataType="text" Length="8" />
<ItemDef OID="ID.AEENMON" SASFieldName="AEENMON"
    Name="Stop Month - Enter Two Digits 01-12" DataType="text"
    Length="2" />
<ItemDef OID="ID.AEENDAY" SASFieldName="AEENDAY"
    Name="Stop Day - Enter Two Digits 01-31" DataType="text"
    Length="2" />
<ItemDef OID="ID.AEENYR" SASFieldName="AEENYR"
    Name="Stop Year - Enter Four Digit Year" DataType="text"
    Length="4" />
<ItemDef OID="ID.AEENDT" SASFieldName="AEENDT"
    Name="Derived Stop Date" DataType="text" Length="8" />
<ItemDef OID="ID.AESEV" SASFieldName="AESEV"
    Name="Severity" DataType="text" Length="1">
    <CodeListRef CodeListOID="CL.$AESEV" />
</ItemDef>
<ItemDef OID="ID.AEREL" SASFieldName="AEREL"
```

```
      Name="Relationship to study drug" DataType="text" Length="1">
       <CodeListRef CodeListOID="CL.$AEREL" />
    </ItemDef>
    <ItemDef OID="ID.AEOUT" SASFieldName="AEOUT" Name="Outcome"
      DataType="text" Length="1">
       <CodeListRef CodeListOID="CL.$AEOUT" />
    </ItemDef>
    <ItemDef OID="ID.AEACTTRT" SASFieldName="AEACTTRT"
      Name="Actions taken re study drug" DataType="text" Length="1">
       <CodeListRef CodeListOID="CL.$AEACTTR" />
    </ItemDef>
    <ItemDef OID="ID.AECONTRT" SASFieldName="AECONTRT"
      Name="Actions taken, other" DataType="text" Length="1">
       <CodeListRef CodeListOID="CL.$AECONTR" />
    </ItemDef>



    <!--
      Translation to ODM markup for any PROC FORMAT style.
      User formatting is applied to columns in the table.
      -->
   <CodeList OID="CL.$TAREAF" SASFormatName="$TAREAF" Name="$TAREAF"
     DataType="text">
      <CodeListItem CodedValue='ONC'>
         <Decode>
            <TranslatedText xml:lang="en">Oncology</TranslatedText>
         </Decode>
      </CodeListItem>
   </CodeList>


   <CodeList OID="CL.$SCTRYF" SASFormatName="$SCTRYF" Name="$SCTRYF"
     DataType="text">
      <CodeListItem CodedValue='USA'>
         <Decode>
           <TranslatedText xml:lang="en">United States</TranslatedText>
         </Decode>
      </CodeListItem>
   </CodeList>


   <CodeList OID="CL.$F_STATU" SASFormatName="$F_STATU" Name="$F_STATU"
      DataType="text">
      <CodeListItem CodedValue='S'>
          <Decode>
           <TranslatedText
            xml:lang="en">Source verified, not queried</TranslatedText>
          </Decode>
      </CodeListItem>
      <CodeListItem CodedValue='V'>
          <Decode>
           <TranslatedText
             xml:lang="en">Source verified, queried</TranslatedText>
          </Decode>
      </CodeListItem>
   </CodeList>
```

```
<CodeList OID="CL.$AESEV" SASFormatName="$AESEV" Name="$AESEV"
   DataType="text">
   <CodeListItem CodedValue='1'>
      <Decode>
         <TranslatedText xml:lang="en">Mild</TranslatedText>
      </Decode>
   </CodeListItem>
 <CodeListItem CodedValue='2'>
      <Decode>
         <TranslatedText xml:lang="en">Moderate</TranslatedText>
      </Decode>
   </CodeListItem>
   <CodeListItem CodedValue='3'>
      <Decode>
         <TranslatedText xml:lang="en">Severe</TranslatedText>
      </Decode>
   </CodeListItem>
   <CodeListItem CodedValue='4'>
      <Decode>
         <TranslatedText
            xml:lang="en">Life Threatening</TranslatedText>
      </Decode>
   </CodeListItem>
</CodeList>

<CodeList OID="CL.$AEREL" SASFormatName="$AEREL" Name="$AEREL"
   DataType="text">
   <CodeListItem CodedValue='0'>
      <Decode>
         <TranslatedText xml:lang="en">None</TranslatedText>
      </Decode>
   </CodeListItem>
 <CodeListItem CodedValue='1'>
      <Decode>
         <TranslatedText xml:lang="en">Unlikely</TranslatedText>
      </Decode>
   </CodeListItem>
   <CodeListItem CodedValue='2'>
      <Decode>
         <TranslatedText xml:lang="en">Possible</TranslatedText>
      </Decode>
   </CodeListItem>
   <CodeListItem CodedValue='3'>
      <Decode>
         <TranslatedText xml:lang="en">Probable</TranslatedText>
      </Decode>
   </CodeListItem>
 </CodeList>

<CodeList OID="CL.$AEOUT" SASFormatName="$AEOUT" Name="$AEOUT"
   DataType="text">
    <CodeListItem CodedValue='1'>
       <Decode>
```

```
            <TranslatedText
              xml:lang="en">Resolved, no residual effects</TranslatedText>
          </Decode>
        </CodeListItem>
        <CodeListItem CodedValue='2'>
          <Decode>
            <TranslatedText xml:lang="en">Continuing</TranslatedText>
          </Decode>
        </CodeListItem>
        <CodeListItem CodedValue='3'>
          <Decode>
            <TranslatedText
              xml:lang="en">Resolved, residual effects</TranslatedText>
          </Decode>
        </CodeListItem>
        <CodeListItem CodedValue='4'>
          <Decode>
            <TranslatedText xml:lang="en">Death</TranslatedText>
          </Decode>
        </CodeListItem>
      </CodeList>

      <CodeList OID="CL.$AEACTTR" SASFormatName="$AEACTTR" Name="$AEACTTR"
        DataType="text">
        <CodeListItem CodedValue='0'>
          <Decode>
            <TranslatedText xml:lang="en">None</TranslatedText>
          </Decode>
        </CodeListItem>
        <CodeListItem CodedValue='1'>
          <Decode>
            <TranslatedText
              xml:lang="en">Discontinued permanently</TranslatedText>
          </Decode>
        </CodeListItem>
        <CodeListItem CodedValue='2'>
          <Decode>
            <TranslatedText xml:lang="en">Reduced</TranslatedText>
          </Decode>
        </CodeListItem>
        <CodeListItem CodedValue='3'>
          <Decode>
            <TranslatedText xml:lang="en">Interrupted</TranslatedText>
          </Decode>
        </CodeListItem>
      </CodeList>

      <CodeList OID="CL.$AECONTR" SASFormatName="$AECONTR"
        Name="$AECONTR" DataType="text">
        <CodeListItem CodedValue='0'>
          <Decode>
            <TranslatedText xml:lang="en">None</TranslatedText>
          </Decode>
        </CodeListItem>
```

```
                    <CodeListItem CodedValue='1'>
                       <Decode>
                         <TranslatedText
                         xml:lang="en">Medication required</TranslatedText>
                       </Decode>
                    </CodeListItem>
                    <CodeListItem CodedValue='2'>
                       <Decode>
                         <TranslatedText
                         xml:lang="en">Hospitalization required or
                         prolonged</TranslatedText>
                       </Decode>
                    </CodeListItem>
                    <CodeListItem CodedValue='3'>
                       <Decode>
                          <TranslatedText xml:lang="en">Other</TranslatedText>
                       </Decode>
                    </CodeListItem>
                </CodeList>
            </MetaDataVersion>
          </Study>


          <!--
                  Administrative metadata
              -->
          <AdminData />


          <!--
                  Clinical Data    : AE
                                     Adverse Events
                                     All adverse events in this trial
              -->
          <ClinicalData StudyOID="123-456-789" MetaDataVersionOID="v1.1.0">
            <SubjectData SubjectKey="001">
               <StudyEventData StudyEventOID="SE.VISIT1">
                  <FormData FormOID="FORM.AE">
                     <ItemGroupData ItemGroupOID="IG.AE" ItemGroupRepeatKey="1"
                        TransactionType="Insert">
                        <ItemData ItemOID="ID.TAREA" Value="ONC"/>
                        <ItemData ItemOID="ID.PNO" Value="143-02"/>
                        <ItemData ItemOID="ID.SCTRY" Value="USA"/>
                        <ItemData ItemOID="ID.F_STATUS" Value="V"/>
                        <ItemData ItemOID="ID.LINE_NO" Value="1"/>
                        <ItemData ItemOID="ID.AETERM" Value="HEADACHE"/>
                        <ItemData ItemOID="ID.AESTMON" Value="06"/>
                        <ItemData ItemOID="ID.AESTDAY" Value="10"/>
                        <ItemData ItemOID="ID.AESTYR" Value="1999"/>
                        <ItemData ItemOID="ID.AESTDT" Value="19990610"/>
                        <ItemData ItemOID="ID.AEENMON" Value="06"/>
                        <ItemData ItemOID="ID.AEENDAY" Value="14"/>
                        <ItemData ItemOID="ID.AEENYR" Value="1999"/>
                        <ItemData ItemOID="ID.AEENDT" Value="19990614"/>
```

```
                    <ItemData ItemOID="ID.AESEV" Value="1"/>
                    <ItemData ItemOID="ID.AEREL" Value="0"/>
                    <ItemData ItemOID="ID.AEOUT" Value="1"/>
                    <ItemData ItemOID="ID.AEACTTRT" Value="0"/>
                    <ItemData ItemOID="ID.AECONTRT" Value="1"/>
                </ItemGroupData>
                <ItemGroupData ItemGroupOID="IG.AE" ItemGroupRepeatKey="2"
                    TransactionType="Insert">
                    <ItemData ItemOID="ID.TAREA" Value="ONC"/>
                    <ItemData ItemOID="ID.PNO" Value="143-02"/>
                    <ItemData ItemOID="ID.SCTRY" Value="USA"/>
                    <ItemData ItemOID="ID.F_STATUS" Value="V"/>
                    <ItemData ItemOID="ID.LINE_NO" Value="2"/>
                    <ItemData ItemOID="ID.AETERM" Value="CONGESTION"/>
                    <ItemData ItemOID="ID.AESTMON" Value="06"/>
                    <ItemData ItemOID="ID.AESTDAY" Value="11"/>
                    <ItemData ItemOID="ID.AESTYR" Value="1999"/>
                    <ItemData ItemOID="ID.AESTDT" Value="19990611"/>
                    <ItemData ItemOID="ID.AEENMON" Value=""/>
                    <ItemData ItemOID="ID.AEENDAY" Value=""/>
                    <ItemData ItemOID="ID.AEENYR" Value=""/>
                    <ItemData ItemOID="ID.AEENDT" Value=""/>
                    <ItemData ItemOID="ID.AESEV" Value="1"/>
                    <ItemData ItemOID="ID.AEREL" Value="0"/>
                    <ItemData ItemOID="ID.AEOUT" Value="2"/>
                    <ItemData ItemOID="ID.AEACTTRT" Value="0"/>
                    <ItemData ItemOID="ID.AECONTRT" Value="1"/>
                </ItemGroupData>
            </FormData>
        </StudyEventData>
      </SubjectData>
    </ClinicalData>
  </ODM>
```

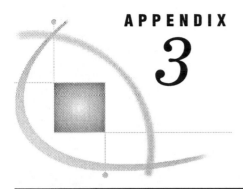

3

Recommended Reading

Recommended Reading

Here is the recommended reading list for this title:

- □ *The Little SAS Book: A Primer*
- □ *SAS Language Reference: Concepts*
- □ *SAS Language Reference: Dictionary*
- □ SAS Companion that is specific to your operating environment
- □ Base SAS Community Web site at **support.sas.com/rnd/base/index.html**
- □ For information about XML (Extensible Markup Language), see the Web site **www.w3.org/XML**

For a complete list of SAS publications, see the current *SAS Publishing Catalog*. To order the most current publications or to receive a free copy of the catalog, contact a SAS representative at

SAS Publishing Sales
SAS Campus Drive
Cary, NC 27513
Telephone: (800) 727-3228*
Fax: (919) 677-8166
E-mail: **sasbook@sas.com**
Web address: **support.sas.com/pubs**
* For other SAS Institute business, call (919) 677-8000.

Customers outside the United States should contact their local SAS office.

Glossary

encoding

a set of characters (letters, logograms, digits, punctuation, symbols, control characters, and so on) that have been mapped to numeric values (called code points) that can be used by computers. The code points are assigned to the characters in the character set by applying an encoding method. Some examples of encodings are wlatin1, wcyrillic, and shift-jis.

fileref (file reference)

a short name (or alias) for the full physical name of an external file. A SAS FILENAME statement maps the fileref to the full physical name.

libref (library reference)

a valid SAS name that serves as a shortcut name to associate with the physical location of an XML document.

markup language

a set of codes that are embedded in text in order to define layout and certain content.

metadata

a description or definition of data or information.

observation

a row in a SAS data set. All of the data values in an observation are associated with a single entity such as a customer or a state. Each observation contains one data value for each variable.

SAS data file

a type of SAS data set that contains data values as well as descriptor information that is associated with the data. The descriptor information includes information such as the data types and lengths of the variables, as well as the name of the engine that was used to create the data. See also SAS data set, SAS data view.

SAS data set

a file whose contents are in one of the native SAS file formats. There are two types of SAS data sets: SAS data files and SAS data views. SAS data files contain data values in addition to descriptor information that is associated with the data. SAS data views contain only the descriptor information plus other information that is required for retrieving data values from other SAS data sets or from files whose contents are in other software vendors' file formats.

SAS data view

a type of SAS data set that retrieves data values from other files. A SAS data view contains only descriptor information such as the data types and lengths of the variables (columns), plus other information that is required for retrieving data values from other SAS data sets or from files that are stored in other software vendors' file formats. SAS data views can be created by the ACCESS and SQL procedures, as well as by the SAS DATA step.

SAS library

one or more SAS files that are accessed by the same library engine and which are referenced and stored as a unit.

SAS XML LIBNAME engine

the SAS engine that processes XML documents. The engine exports an XML document from a SAS data set by translating the proprietary SAS file format to XML markup. The engine also imports an external XML document by translating XML markup to a SAS data set.

SAS XML Mapper

a graphical interface that you can use to create and modify XMLMaps for use by the SAS XML LIBNAME engine. The SAS XML Mapper analyzes the structure of an XML document or an XML schema and generates basic XML markup for the XMLMap.

variable

a column in a SAS data set or in a SAS data view. The data values for each variable describe a single characteristic for all observations.

XML (Extensible Markup Language)

a markup language that structures information by tagging it for content, meaning, or use. Structured information contains both content (for example, words or numbers) and an indication of what role the content plays. For example, content in a section heading has a different meaning from content in a database table.

XML engine

See SAS XML LIBNAME engine.

XMLMap

a file that contains XML tags that tell the SAS XML LIBNAME engine how to interpret an XML document.

Index

Your Turn

If you have comments or suggestions about *SAS® 9.1.3 XML LIBNAME Engine: User's Guide*, please send them to us on a photocopy of this page, or send us electronic mail.

For comments about this book, please return the photocopy to

SAS Publishing
SAS Campus Drive
Cary, NC 27513
E-mail: **yourturn@sas.com**

For suggestions about the software, please return the photocopy to

SAS Institute Inc.
Technical Support Division
SAS Campus Drive
Cary, NC 27513
E-mail: **suggest@sas.com**

9 781590 475225